BRAIN BASED STRESS MANAGEMENT

by
An Swinnen

BRAIN BASED STRESS MANAGEMENT
by An Swinnen

Copyright © 2019 by An Swinnen

All Rights Reserved.

The use of any part of this publication reproduced, transmitted in any form or by any means, electronic, mechanical, recording or otherwise, or stored in a retrieval system, without the prior written permission of the publisher is an infringement of the copyright law. Any request for photocopying, recording, or for storing of information and retrieval systems of any art of this book should be directed in writing to *info@becsltd.com*.

The information given in this book should not be treated as a substitute for professional medical advice. Individuals should always consult a medical practitioner. Any use of the information presented in this book is at the reader's discretion and risk. Neither the author nor the publishers can be held responsible for any loss, claim or damage arising out of the use, or misuse, of the suggestions made, the failure to take medical advice or for any material on third party websites.

Proofread and Edited by Dr Bridget Andrews

Cover Design and Illustrations by Dusan Arsenic

Editorial Design by Lazar Kackarovski

Printed and Bound by CLOC London

ISBN: 978-0-9567007-1-1

Published 2019 by Business English Consulting Service Ltd,
126 Aldersgate Street, London EC1A 4JQ

To everyone
who made it possible
for me to write this book

TABLE OF CONTENTS

Welcome! 9

Introduction 10

CHAPTER 1: Stress 13
   What is Stress? 14
   Is Stress Dangerous? 15
   Stress Symptoms 17
   Questionnaire: Are you Stressed at Work? 19

CHAPTER 2: How Does the Brain Work? 23
   The Intellectual Brain 24
      a. The Pre-Frontal Cortex – The Intellectual Boss   25
      b. The Default Network Mode – The Intellectual Daydreamer   27
   The Primitive Brain 29
      a. The Amygdala – Your Bodyguard   31
      b. The Hippocampus – Your Filing Cabinet   32
      c. The Hypothalamus – Your Chemist   33
      d. The "I am Fantastic" Technique   34
   The Primitive Brain's Opt Out Clauses 35
      a. Depression   35
      b. Anxiety   37
      c. Anger   40

Your Stress Bucket 43

REM Sleep Empties your Stress Bucket 45

Why Do We Sleep? 47

Why Do We Dream? 51

Serotonin and Your Stress Bucket 53

How Do We Produce Serotonin? 54
    a. Positive Action   54
    b. Positive Interaction   54
    c. Positive Thoughts   54
    d. Other Methods of Producing Serotonin   55

Why am I Self-Destructive? 57

CHAPTER 3:   Helping the Brain 61

Exercise 62

Brain Foods 66

The Importance of Touch 76

The Effect of Music 79

Nature 84

Meditation 87

Laughter 90

The Internet 92

Smoking 98

Drugs 101

Table of Contents

CHAPTER 4:   Why Do Others Stress Me Out? *105*
  *Personality Types and Their Influence
      on Your Stress Bucket* *106*
  Characteristics of the Four DISC Types *108*
  Identifying DISC Personalities. *112*
  Your Online DISC Personality Test *114*
  Adapting Your Behaviour to Influence Others *116*

CHAPTER 5:   How Do I Solve My Problems? *123*

CHAPTER 6:   Why Can't I Change? *127*
  The ADKAR Technique *128*

CHAPTER 7;   Dealing with Big Changes and Loss *135*
  Kubler-Ross Change Curve *136*

CHAPTER 8:   Self Help Planner *145*

What I Got From This Book *174*

Acknowledgements *175*

Relaxation Recording *177*

WELCOME!

WELCOME TO THE FIRST day of the rest of your happier and healthier life!

Finding out how the brain works is a real revelation. This book teaches you that you are in control over how you feel. You are the boss. Your brain will follow your lead. All the techniques and tips are free and fun.

The book includes puzzles, word searches, as well as spaces for you to draw, colour in and plan. Get stuck in and enjoy your journey!

This book belongs to:

INTRODUCTION

WRITING THIS BOOK WOULD not have been possible without the hard work of many neurologists, psychologists, psychiatrists, psychotherapists, doctors, scientists, researchers, authors, universities, hospitals, Ministries of Health and other organisations dedicated to understanding the brain and making us feel better. I have included a very long list of acknowledgements at the back of the book.

I would not have written the book without David Newman of CPHT Bristol and Matthew Cahill and Joanne Welsh of CPHT Plymouth. David Newman and his team analysed years of psychological and neurological research and did all the hard work. Matthew Cahill, who has a successful practice in Harley Street in London, very patiently taught me the diploma course which David designed and Joanne was in the background supervising my progress. Thanks also to Dr Bridget Andrews for proofreading and editing. Dr Bridget has a MSc in Foundations of Clinical Neuropsychology and PhD in Cognitive Neuroscience.

As Managing Director of BECS, a corporate training company based in London, I meet with many HR and Training Managers. Stress Management is a very popular course as absenteeism at work is a big problem. Many schools and hospitals run on supply staff because so many employees are off work with depression or anxiety. The media is full of mental health, burnout and suicide stories.

Introduction

I realised that the average stress management course only treats the symptoms but not the causes. As part of my teaching degree I studied educational psychology. All the BECS courses are designed with brain based learning in mind, and so is this book. If I wanted to get to the core of the stress problem, I had to study the brain and find out what causes depression, anxiety, anger and burnouts. More importantly, I had to find ways of tricking the brain into feeling happier and healthier.

I did not want to go back to university to study psychology for four years. I was much too busy running BECS. A psychology degree includes too much theory and history, something I had already covered in my education degree. I wanted a clinical course that would focus on the psychology of mental health problems. After a lot of research I found an accredited diploma course at CPHT Plymouth: "Clinical Solution-Focused Hypnotherapy and Psychotherapy". I signed up and never looked back.

This book is designed to be positive, fun, easy, practical and thought-provoking. It is your guide to a better future. It includes a relaxation recording (see the last page) and a self help planner at the back of the book. You can use the planner on your own, with a friend, partner or parent. If you would like to work with a stress management coach, just let us know. We can help. Just send an email to *info@becsltd.com*.

CHAPTER 1
STRESS

WHAT IS STRESS?

We all talk about stress and feeling stressed, when we feel we have too much to do and too much on our minds. Sometimes other people are making unreasonable demands on us, or we are dealing with situations that we do not have control over.

Severe stress that continues for a long time may lead to a medical diagnosis of depression, anxiety or more severe mental and general health problems such as heart attacks, strokes and diabetes.

You can reduce the effects of stress by being more conscious of the causes, and learning to handle them better, using relaxation techniques as well as other lifestyle changes described in this book.

IS STRESS DANGEROUS?

STRESS CAN HAVE A positive side. A certain level of stress may be necessary and enjoyable in order to help you prepare for something or to actually do it, e.g. if you are taking part in a performance, taking an exam or you have to complete an important piece of work with an imminent deadline. It will be stressful even if you enjoy it, and the stress itself will keep you alert and focused.

Our physical reactions to stress are determined by our biological history and the need to respond to sudden dangers that threatened us when we were still cavemen. In this situation, the response to danger was 'fight, flight or freeze'. Our bodies still respond in this way, releasing the hormones adrenaline and cortisol.

ADRENALINE

The release of adrenaline causes rapid changes to your blood flow and increases your breathing and heart rate, to get you ready to defend yourself (fight) or to run away (flight). You become pale, sweat more and your mouth becomes dry.

Your body responds in this way to all types of stress as if it were a physical threat. When you have an argument with someone, your body may react as though you were facing a wolf. If the threat is physical and real, you use the effects of the adrenaline appropriately. You fight or run. When the danger has passed, your body recovers.

If the stress is emotional, the effects of adrenaline subside more slowly, and you may continue to feel agitated for a long time. If the causes of stress are long-term, you may always be tensed up in order to deal with them and therefor never relaxed. This is very bad for both your physical and your mental health.

CORTISOL

The other stress hormone, cortisol, is present in your body all the time but levels increase in response to danger and stress. In the short-term, its effects are positive, to help you deal with an immediate crisis; but long-term stress causes cortisol to build up, creating a number of stress-related health problems.

Short-Term Positive Effects:

- Quick burst of energy
- Decreased sensitivity to pain
- Increase in immunity
- Heightened memory

Long-Term Negative Effects:

- Imbalances of blood sugar
- Increase in abdominal fat storage
- Suppressed thyroid activity
- Decreased bone density
- Decreased muscle mass
- High blood pressure
- Lowered immunity
- Lowered ability to think clearly

People's tolerance of stress varies. A situation that is intolerable to one person may be stimulating to another. What you feel is determined not just by events and changes in the outside world, but how you perceive, think about and respond to them.

The important point is that you can learn to recognise your own responses to stress and develop skills to deal with it well.

STRESS SYMPTOMS

HOW YOUR BODY MAY REACT: TICK IF YOU ARE AFFECTED

- Fast shallow breathing ☐
- Headaches ☐
- Constant tiredness ☐
- Restlessness ☐
- Sleeping problems ☐
- Tendency to sweat ☐
- Nervous twitches ☐
- Cramps or muscle spasms ☐
- Pins and needles ☐
- High blood pressure ☐
- Feeling sick or dizzy ☐
- Constipation or diarrhoea ☐
- Craving for food ☐
- Indigestion or heartburn ☐
- Lack of appetite ☐
- Chest pains ☐
- Grinding your teeth at night ☐

HOW YOU MAY FEEL:

- Irritable ☐
- Aggressive ☐
- Depressed ☐
- Fearing failure ☐
- Dreading the future ☐
- Loss of interest in others ☐
- Taking no interest in life ☐
- Neglected ☐
- That there's no one to confide in ☐
- Loss of sense of humour ☐
- Bad or ugly ☐
- Fearful that you are seriously ill ☐

HOW YOU MAY BEHAVE:

- Finding it difficult to make decisions ☐
- Finding it difficult to concentrate ☐
- Denying there's a problem ☐
- Avoiding difficult situations ☐
- Frequently crying ☐
- Biting your nails ☐
- Unable to show your true feelings ☐
- Being very snappy or aggressive ☐
- Finding it difficult to talk to others ☐

QUESTIONNAIRE: ARE YOU STRESSED AT WORK?

	Question	Not at All	Rarely	Some times	Often	Very Often
1	Do you feel run down and drained of physical or emotional energy?	☐	☐	☐	☐	☐
2	Do you find that you think negatively about your job?	☐	☐	☐	☐	☐
3	Do you find that you are harder and less sympathetic with people than perhaps they deserve?	☐	☐	☐	☐	☐
4	Do you find yourself getting easily irritated by small problems, or by your colleagues and team?	☐	☐	☐	☐	☐

	Question	Not at All	Rarely	Some times	Often	Very Often
5	Do you feel misunderstood or unappreciated by your colleagues?	☐	☐	☐	☐	☐
6	Do you feel that you have no one to talk to?	☐	☐	☐	☐	☐
7	Do you feel that you are achieving less than you should?	☐	☐	☐	☐	☐
8	Do you feel under an unpleasant level of pressure to succeed?	☐	☐	☐	☐	☐
9	Do you feel that you are not getting what you want out of your job?	☐	☐	☐	☐	☐
10	Do you feel that you are in the wrong organisation or the wrong profession?	☐	☐	☐	☐	☐
11	Are you becoming frustrated with parts of your job?	☐	☐	☐	☐	☐

Questionnaire: Are you Stressed at Work?

	Question	Not at All	Rarely	Some times	Often	Very Often
12	Do you feel that organisational politics or bureaucracy frustrate your ability to do a good job?	☐	☐	☐	☐	☐
13	Do you feel that there is more work to do than you practically have the ability to do?	☐	☐	☐	☐	☐
14	Do you feel that you do not have time to do many of the things that are important to doing a good quality job?	☐	☐	☐	☐	☐
15	Do you find that you do not have time to plan as much as you would like to?	☐	☐	☐	☐	☐

* *For each statement decide how true it is for you. Award yourself 1 point for each "Not at All"; answer 2 for "Rarely"; 3 for "Sometimes"; 4 for "Often" and 5 for "Very Often".*

** *Then add up your total score and check on the next page:*

STRESS SCORE INTERPRETATION

- 15-18 There are no signs of stress.
- 19-32 Little sign of stress, unless some factors are particularly severe.
- 33-49 Be careful. You may be at risk of stress, particularly if several scores are high.
- 50-59 You are at severe risk of high stress. Do something about this urgently.
- 60-75 You are at very severe risk of burnout. Do something about this urgently.

"But on the positive side, money can't buy happiness - so who cares?"

CHAPTER 2
HOW DOES THE BRAIN WORK?

THE INTELLECTUAL BRAIN

THE INTELLECTUAL BRAIN IS the brain you know as you. It is your conscious part that interacts with the world.

At the moment it is attached to a vast intellectual resource, the main cortex of the brain. This part we do not share with other animals. Humans can think in the past, present and future. Animals can only think in the past and present. Thinking in the future is very important and means that we have evolved so much more than animals.

When we operate from the intellectual part of the brain we generally get things right in life. It will always come up with answers based on a proper assessment of the situation and is generally very positive. We will look at all sides of a problem in a calm manner and come up with some creative solutions.

A. THE PRE-FRONTAL CORTEX – THE INTELLECTUAL BOSS

The pre-frontal cortex is the most important part of our intellectual brain.

Our brains are bombarded with enormous amounts of information from the outside world every second. All of this information is then mingled with previous knowledge and the goals that we want to achieve. One of the most complex tasks for our brains is to make order and sense out of all these things.

The brain has a special system to control the flow of information, how the information is processed and how to achieve our goals. These are called executive functions and occur mostly in the pre-frontal cortex of the brain. With an active pre-frontal cortex we can achieve our overall goals by changing the rules in order to adapt to a constantly changing environment.

Within the pre-frontal cortex we can suppress processes that are incompatible with our goals and we can also boost other processes that are important for achieving what we want. This type of regulation is important when processing multiple pieces of information at the same time or when things are happening quickly. In a way a boss is like the pre-frontal cortex: regulating rewards, clarifying competing priorities, diverting resources accordingly for multiple tasks and seeing what is not important.

How easily a boss can meet the demands of their job is based very much on their executive functions. Bosses need to be focused on the overall goal in all information processing. They will have many parallel flows of information online simultaneously, and need to extract and integrate the important points out of this flow that will lead to the desired goal. At the same time they must suppress distracting pieces of information that are not moving towards their goal. Every time something changes in the context they quickly build new rules to achieve the goal in a creative way.

Thankfully the boss can intervene when our brain starts functioning in the emotional, primitive part of our brain which is quite negative and cannot rationalise. The pre-frontal cortex is in charge (except when you are in a physical dangerous situation such as a fire or tsunami and your survival instinct takes over).

B. THE DEFAULT NETWORK MODE – THE INTELLECTUAL DAYDREAMER

Thomas Edison, the famous scientist, had an interesting work method. He would often have a break from work, sit in a chair and relax with a few small balls in his hand. He opened his default network mode to let his mind wander. If he started dozing, the balls would drop noisily on the floor and keep him from sleeping. These breaks often lead to deep insights, AHA! moments or magical solutions to problems. Apparently Salvador Dali the famous, eccentric artist also had a similar routine. In Dali's case it led to amazing creativity.

According to Dr Barbara Oakley, Professor of Engineering at Oakland University, these men were engaging the default network mode which lies in the intellectual part of our brain.

> *"Since the very beginning of the 21st century, neuroscientists have been making profound advances in understanding the two different types of networks that the brain switches between—highly attentive states and more relaxed default mode networks. We'll call the thinking processes related to these networks the focused mode and diffuse mode, respectively—these modes are highly important for learning. It seems you frequently switch back and forth between these two modes in your day-to-day activities. You're in either one mode or the other—not consciously in both at the same time. The diffuse mode does seem to be able to work quietly in the background on something you are not actively focusing on. Sometimes you may also flicker for a rapid moment to diffuse mode thinking.",*
> **Barbara Oakley via Science Friday**

Just like Edison, we too can and should benefit from using our default network mode. Daydreaming helps us to see the big picture. It is also in this mode that the brain makes connections among disparate things which we may have gathered while using the pre-frontal cortex. These disparate connections give rise to AHA! moments and what often seems like magical solutions to difficult problems.

If you cannot solve a problem, STOP! Go for a walk, ring a friend, watch some television or go for a run. Take yourself away from the problem and do something you like. Your subconscious intellectual brain is working in the background, although you do not realise this. That is why you come up with the answer of a difficult exam question while driving home.

Daydreaming is great for trying out possible outcomes of an action in the safety of your own brain. If you would like to tell your boss you are leaving, the diffuse mode of your brain will allow you to rehearse for this safely.

THE PRIMITIVE BRAIN

There is another part of the brain. This part is the original primitive part which we share with animals. The primitive part makes sure that we stay alive: it makes our heart beat, lungs pump and organs function. In physical danger it will switch our body into survival mode to keep us alive.

The primitive mind is a negative mind. It will always see things from the worst possible perspective. It has to for your self-preservation. When you run into a wolf, it will not say "Let's think about this logically. The wolf has probably already eaten". Instead, your brain will say: "It will kill you". This response is great when we run into wolves but not so good when the bank statement arrives, we are facing redundancy or we have had an argument.

The primitive mind is an obsessional mind. If you have a wolf in the back garden you will be reminded of it constantly. You would keep checking. You would become obsessed about the wolf and think about it constantly. That is why a family argument or money problems can be on your mind for weeks.

It is a vigilant mind. If the perception is that danger is all around, then it is wise to stay on red alert which increases your anxiety levels.

Because the primitive brain is not an intellectual brain, it can't be innovative. It has to refer to previous patterns of behaviour. If what we did yesterday ensured our survival then we are encouraged to do it again, even if the behaviour is self-destructive, e.g. drugs, gambling, binging and smoking.

The primitive brain includes:

- the amygdala
- the hippocampus
- the hypothalamus

A. THE AMYGDALA – YOUR BODYGUARD

The almond-shaped central part of the primitive brain is the amygdala. This is generally referred to as the fight/flight/freeze area of the brain.

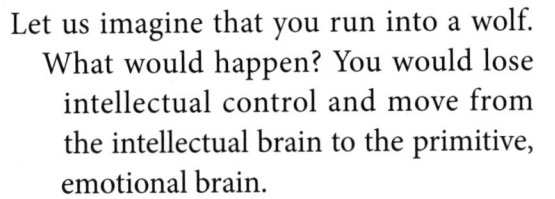

Let us imagine that you run into a wolf. What would happen? You would lose intellectual control and move from the intellectual brain to the primitive, emotional brain.

The amygdala picks up information from our senses. The amygdala always thinks that everything and everyone is going to kill us: the air, the people, the car, the cupboard and the wolf. Thankfully the amygdala does not react immediately because otherwise we would be in a continuous state of complete panic. Instead, it will send a message to the hippocampus, our filing cabinet, to say that there is a wolf and then wait for instructions.

B. THE HIPPOCAMPUS – YOUR FILING CABINET

The hippocampus has a unique shape, similar to that of a horseshoe. It not only assists with the storage of long term memories, but is also responsible for the memory of the location of objects or people. We would not even be able to remember where our house is without the work of the hippocampus. Alzheimer's disease has been proven to have affected and damaged this area of the brain.

The hippocampus holds information on what we have read, seen, smelled, heard and felt.

The hippocampus will look up information on a potential threat and tell the amygdala if the threat is real and what the best reaction would be, according to what is in the filing cabinet.

The hippocampus will check what we know about wolves and if it is a danger to us. The hippocampus realises that the wolf is very dangerous and that the best response out of the fight/flight/freeze option is to flight and run as hard as you can. It will send this information back to the amygdala.

C. THE HYPOTHALAMUS – YOUR CHEMIST

The hypothalamus regulates our chemical responses in the body and mind.

If the hippocampus confirms to the amygdala that there is a danger and sends instructions for how we should react, the amygdala will send a message to the hypothalamus which will produce a lot of stress hormones such as adrenaline and cortisol so you can run faster. You go sweaty, your heart rate increases, your stomach churns and you are off like a shot. The primitive brain did its job and kept you alive.

If you want to lower the stress hormones in your body, take deep breaths. The oxygen in your blood helps lower them.

D. THE "I AM FANTASTIC" TECHNIQUE

The primitive brain cannot distinguish reality from imagination. That is why you become anxious, your heart rate goes up and you start sweating when you watch a horror movie. Your primitive brain does not realise that the film is fiction and will respond as if you are being chased by a crazy murderer.

You can use this to your advantage. Whatever you tell your primitive brain, it will be stored in the hippocampus as the truth. The more times you repeat "I am fantastic", the stronger the neural pathway will be in your brain and the fact that you are fantastic becomes the truth, thus making you more self-confident and calm under pressure.

Listen to the relaxation recording on the last page. It will relax you, make you calm and build your self-confidence. Your brain will be listening to my voice telling it that you are fantastic.

Repeat "I am fantastic" many times, especially when you feel very relaxed. You are more open to suggestion when you are relaxed.

Put positive signs up in your house, e.g. "I can do this, I am wonderful, I am fantastic!" A dream board with all your goals is also a good idea. Cut out photos and make it really colourful. Your brain thinks in images (not words) and loves colour. Your pre-frontal cortex arranges your life in order to achieve its goals. The hippocampus will store this information every time it is reminded of your goals.

THE PRIMITIVE BRAIN'S OPT OUT CLAUSES

WHEN OUR ANXIETY GOES up, and it can be a gradual process, we lose intellectual control and the primitive mind takes over. This mind always operates within the primitive parameters of depression, anxiety and anger or a combination of all three.

If our primitive mind thinks that our life is in some sort of crisis or emergency it will step in to help. Depression, anxiety, and anger are all primitive opt out clauses. We can explain them by going back to our roots, the caveman.

A. DEPRESSION

When the caveman looked out of the cave and there was snow, ice, floods or danger, he could not go out to hunt so he pulled the rug over his head and did not come out until the situation changed. We have adapted this to all the modern day symptoms of depression.

When you are depressed, you cannot get out of bed. You pull the duvet over your head and go back to sleep. Sometimes, you do not want to leave the house, go to work or meet up with friends. You feel unmotivated and very low. Your whole system slows down. You feel a deep sadness or emptiness that stays around for a long time, for weeks or longer.

Doctors look for these criteria to help with diagnosis:

- Feeling continually low and hopeless
- Losing enjoyment and interest in things
- Feeling grumpy or irritable a lot of the time
- Being tearful and upset
- Feeling constantly exhausted
- Having trouble sleeping or sleeping too much
- Not being able to concentrate
- Having no appetite or eating too much
- Losing perspective on things
- Thinking of death

Five or more of the symptoms have to be experienced during the same two-week period to be part of a depression diagnosis. At least one of the symptoms has to be either feeling low and hopeless or loss of enjoyment and interest.

Depression Management Techniques

- Use The Swinnen Technique on page 42
- Do not withdraw from life.
- Be active. You will feel better.
- Go out into nature and enjoy the weather.
- Do not drink alcohol. It dehydrates your body and brain and you will feel miserable afterwards. Alcohol stops the production of serotonin, a neurotransmitter which gets you into a good mood.
- Have a routine.
- Listen to the relaxation recording on the last page. Sit back and relax.

B. ANXIETY

If the caveman was in a jungle with all its sounds and movements, he would not be too far away from his panic button. The amygdala, hippocampus and hypothalamus would be in overdrive and produce a lot of stress hormones such as adrenaline and cortisol.

People with anxiety problems feel anxious almost all of the time and worrying significantly affects their lives. The anxiety finds something to worry about, even if there is nothing scary or going wrong. They feel afraid, panicky, anxious, worried and nervous almost all the time.

Symptoms of Anxiety:

- Shortness of breath
- Nightmares
- Difficulty swallowing
- Feelings of dread
- Tense muscles
- Inability to sleep
- Crying
- Headache
- Fidgeting
- Sweating
- Shaking

Types of Anxiety:

- **Generalised Anxiety:** worrying excessively about anything and everything including your job, exams, family, friends, health and relationships.
- **Separation Anxiety:** finding it hard to leave your loved ones and feeling very nervous when you are without them.
- **Social Anxiety:** this happens when normal nervousness in social situations becomes intense and overwhelming, e.g. going out, answering the phone, seeing other people.

The Calm Technique

This is a technique that tricks your brain into feeling very calm quickly:

1. Remember a time when you were very calm. Maybe you were lying on a beach in the sun or under a tree and you were listening to the birds? If you cannot remember a time, just imagine what it would feel like to fully relax and be calm. How good would that feel?
2. Hold on to that thought and maximise the memory in your head: you are even calmer, the sun is even warmer, the sounds brighter, the colours more vivid etc.
3. Keep thinking about this maximised memory. Repeat it 5 times. Each time when you do, combine it with a physical act which will act as a trigger, e.g. turn your ring or squeeze the thumb and middle finger together or touch your earring, etc.
4. Over the next few days keep thinking of the maximised calm memory combined with the physical trigger. The more you repeat this, the more the calm sensation and trigger are programmed into your brain.
5. When you feel anxious or stressed, just use the trigger and your brain will automatically make your body feel very calm.

You can also listen to the relaxation recording on the last page of the book. Sit back and relax.

C. ANGER

Anger is a primitive way of increasing your strength to defend yourself against wild animals, wild tribesman and threats. The hormones adrenaline, cortisol and testosterone released by the hypothalamus, your chemist, make you stronger and that is why fights can end with fatal consequences.

Anger changes your face. It tenses your muscles and makes you scowl. You might also start to talk more quickly and loudly. These external signs of anger are a sign to others to tread carefully.

Anger Management Technique:
1. Walk away from the situation.
2. Take five deep breaths (oxygen lowers your stress hormones).
3. Use The Swinnen Technique on page 42 so your intellectual brain is back in control.
4. Think of possible solutions.

How do You Move from the Primitive Brain to the Intellectual Brain?

You want to be functioning in the intellectual brain which is a positive brain and can think rationally. The Swinnen Technique is a fun and easy technique so you can switch quickly and easily.

The Swinnen Technique

1. Imagine what your amygdala looks like. Draw it here:

[ ]

2. Imagine your amygdala standing on top of your brain.

3. Imagine what your intellectual brain looks like. Draw it here:

4. Imagine your intellectual brain at the bottom of your brain.
5. Take three deep breaths.
6. Think of a way in which the intellectual brain can defeat the amygdala and send it back to the bottom of your brain where it belongs. Each time you do this, you will have to imagine a different method (Think of Tom and Jerry. Tom was very creative in finding new ways to catch Jerry.). The intellectual brain can trick the primitive brain somehow, beat him with a baseball bat, use a lasso, etc.
7. Imagine your intellectual brain as the winner, celebrating at the top of your brain.
8. Smile!

YOUR STRESS BUCKET

Dr Don Clifton was teaching psychology at the University of Nebraska when he created a simple metaphor to describe how we deal with stress. He called it the stress bucket.

This is a very simple idea. Each person has a stress bucket in their head. When you wake up in the morning there is no or a small amount of stress in your bucket. When the day progresses you put more in your bucket.

What exactly goes into the bucket? It is not the events in your lives that necessarily cause the perception of crisis and negative stress. One man's horror is another's man pleasurable challenge, e.g. students have the same professors, workload, deadlines and exams. Some students suffer from panic attacks and some cope very well and flourish. The same goes for doctors and teachers. That is why supply staff who take over their workload, might not have the same mental health problems.

It is not so much the life events that fill up our stress bucket but our thought patterns surrounding the events. Every negative thought we have is converted into anxiety. We can create anxiety by negatively forecasting the future, e.g. "we will never be able to afford that, I'll never find a job, she is going to sack me, I'll never find another girlfriend, the presentation will be terrible".

The primitive mind cannot tell the difference between imagination and reality. Intellectually you know the presentation is going to be fine but you start thinking about everything going wrong. You think about it all the time. The actual presentation goes quite well but in your mind you have delivered 51 presentations and 50 have been disasters.

We can negatively introspect about the past as well e.g. "Why did my husband not come home straight away? Does he still love me?", "Why did my colleague not say anything? Does she hate me?"

Every negative thought that we have is accumulated and stored in our stress bucket. As long as the stress bucket is not overflowing we are fine and we can cope with life. When the stress bucket overflows, we are at risk of depression, anxiety and anger. If the stress bucket overflows for a long period, you might suffer from burnout which has long-term health effects.

REM SLEEP EMPTIES YOUR STRESS BUCKET

THANKFULLY, WE HAVE A method for emptying our stress bucket each night and it is known as REM (Rapid Eye Movement) sleep. At night we re-run events of the day and change them from being an emotional memory to a narrative memory i.e. a memory we have control over in the intellectual brain.

How does REM sleep help? Just imagine someone upsets you in the afternoon. You tell your husband and he tells you to forget about it but you cannot. You are thinking about it when you go to bed. During your REM sleep you will re-run the event either in clear or metaphorical (dreaming) language, and you will move it from the primitive brain to the intellectual brain where you have control over it. When you wake up in the morning you might have forgotten about the argument or you wonder why that person upset you so much.

When you empty your stress bucket in the REM sleep, you wake up each morning feeling ready to take on the world. You can start the day without anxiety, anger or depression.

If you do not wake up with an empty stress bucket in the morning there could be two reasons:

Reason 1

You have been piling too much into your stress bucket and sometimes it will overflow. Sadly, REM sleep is restricted to about 20% of our sleep patterns. If you go over, the mind will wake you up in the middle of the night. You know when it is your mind waking you up because you are wide awake and often feel quite miserable. Often you cannot get back to sleep again.

Now you are in the grip of a bit of a vicious circle. The more you have in your bucket, the more time you will spend in your primitive brain and the more you will be encouraged to be negative.

You need to restrict the amount you are piling into your bucket and concentrate on the positive things in life. You will know when you are doing this when you start sleeping better.

Reason 2

You have been piling too much into your bucket and it takes a great deal of effort to attempt to empty it. Sadly REM sleep is tiring. It requires enormous energy to diffuse that anxiety. Sometimes you can overdo it and this exhausts you and makes you even more depressed.

Now you find yourself in the grip of a vicious circle. In an attempt to empty your stress bucket you are encouraged to sleep more and more, sometimes all day, which makes your depression and anxiety even worse.

You need to restrict the amount you are piling into your bucket and concentrate on the positive aspects in your life.

WHY DO WE SLEEP?

EVERY NIGHT PEOPLE ACROSS the world climb into their beds and shut down for hours. Up until the 1950s, it was widely believed that sleep was just a passive period of unconscious rest, but now we know that it is a complex process that is essential to the rejuvenation of the body and mind.

During sleep, the body moves through five different stages of both REM (rapid eye movement) and NREM (non-rapid eye movement) sleep. Over the course of the night, the body will go through this five-stage cycle four to six times, spending an average of 90 minutes in each stage.

Each stage of sleep serves a unique restorative function, including muscle recovery, hormone regulation, and memory consolidation, making it essential to allow enough time to cycle through all sleep stages. Without a full night of sleep, your body and mind are deprived of the essential elements needed to help you conquer the day.

STAGE ONE

Stage one of sleep, also known as the transitional phase, occurs when you find yourself floating in and out of consciousness. During this NREM stage, you may be partially awake while your mind begins to drift off.

This period of drowsiness eventually leads to a light sleep. This is also the time when the muscles jerk, followed by a falling sensation that jolts you back into consciousness. After winding down in stage one, your sleep cycle will move into stage two.

STAGE TWO

Almost 50% of the time spent asleep over the course of the night is spent in stage two. Stage two is also a non-REM phase and is one of the lighter stages of sleep. Even though it is a light stage, the heart rate begins to slow and the core body temperature decreases.

During stage two, eye movement stops and brain waves slow with the occasional burst of waves called sleep spindles. Stage two can also be characterized by the unstructured periods that alternate between muscle tone and muscle relaxation.

STAGES THREE AND FOUR

Stages three and four are characterized as the deep stages of sleep and are often the hardest to wake up from. If you try to wake someone up when they are in stages three or four, they will most likely be disoriented and groggy for minutes after they awake. Stages three and four are often grouped together because they are the periods of slow wave sleep.

Slow wave sleep is a NREM phase of sleep, and is the deepest sleep that your body enters throughout the night. It is called slow wave sleep because the brain waves slow to what are known as delta waves with the occasional faster wave. As the body transitions from stage three to stage four, the number of delta waves increase and the faster waves decrease.

In addition to the deep sleep caused by the delta waves, blood pressure drops even further, and breathing becomes deeper, slower, and more rhythmic. During slow wave sleep there is no eye movement and the body becomes immobile. However, even though there is no muscle movement, the muscles still have the ability to function. These are the stages when children sometimes experience nightmares, bedwetting and sleepwalking.

Stages three and four of sleep are extremely rejuvenating to the body. During slow wave sleep, hormones are released that aid in both growth and appetite control. The growth hormones help to replenish muscles and tissues that were exerted over the course of the day, and the appetite controlling hormones help limit feelings of excessive hunger the following day.

These hormones are essential to the development of a strong body and help control unnecessary over-eating. In addition to the release of critical hormones, the blood flow to the muscles increases, providing restorative oxygen and nutrients. The body heals itself.

STAGE FIVE

Stage five is the only stage of REM, and is unlike any other sleep phase because the brain is bursting with activity. Most adults spend about 20% of sleep in REM, while infants spend almost 50%. During non-REM sleep, the mind rests while the body heals, but in REM sleep the mind energises itself while the body is immobile.

REM sleep is called as such because the eyes dart in various directions while the limbs and muscles are temporarily paralysed. Breathing becomes shallower and irregular while the heart rate and blood pressure rise from the levels they were in previous stages.

Most dreaming takes place in stage five as a result of heightened, desynchronized brain waves, almost similar to being awake. This stage of sleep revitalises the brain, supporting sharp and alert daytime function.

Individuals begin waking up at the end of stage five. Upon waking up, an individual's core body temperature begins to rise in order to prepare the body for the activity of the day ahead. If it is not morning yet, the body goes back into stage one. Very often you will not remember waking up.

SLEEPING TECHNIQUES

- Listen to the relaxation recording on the last page before you fall asleep. The recording will slow down your body and make sure it gets the right kind of sleep. It will also make you calmer and feel more self-confident.
- Make sure your bedroom is very dark at night. The blue light of routers and TVs make your brain think it is daylight and will wake you up.
- Have a sleeping routine (very useful with children).
- Do not drink coffee in the evening.
- Exercise during the day.
- Make sure you have a good mattress. You should replace it every seven years.
- Do a body scan while you are in bed. Tense each part of your body and then let go so it is totally relaxed. Start with your head and move down to your toes.

WHY DO WE DREAM?

I F WE LET OFF steam when we are angry, we feel better. That is why some people take up boxing. In this society we cannot act on our emotions like cavemen can. If our boss makes us angry, we cannot beat them up in the middle of the office, even if that makes us feel a lot better. We needed to evolve the ability to act on our emotions when necessary and deactivate them later when we could do no harm. That is why we evolved to dream.

During REM sleep unfulfilled emotions from the day are acted out in the form of metaphors in dreams, e.g. a clock is a symbol for time. That way you deactivate those emotions and free up the brain to deal with the new emotions of the following day. Let us go back to our example. Your boss makes you angry at work. Instead of beating them up at the office during the day, you safely beat them up in your dream. You now feel satisfied and the matter is resolved.

You only dream about unresolved issues and emotions from the day before, freeing you up to start the day afresh. If you dreamt about something that happened a long time ago, it means that something happened the day before that triggered that memory.

Why Do We Dream?

DREAM ANALYSIS

Write down your dreams here. Think about your unresolved issues and emotions of the day before. What did your dream mean?

SEROTONIN AND YOUR STRESS BUCKET

CAVEMEN AND WOMEN WERE given rewards for carrying out certain evolutionary processes. They got a reward when they hunted and gathered, and successfully supported themselves and their families. We are better as a tribe than individuals, so they were rewarded when they interacted with others. This reward has been recognised by scientists. It is a chemical response in the brain that produces various neurotransmitters that act as catalysts for mentally healthy behaviour. It helped them cope with day to day activities, physical fear and pain. It made them braver.

The most important neurotransmitter is serotonin. Serotonin regulates our general mood and appetite. When we produce a constant flow of serotonin we are nice, happy, coping, brave people which mean that we do not fill up our stress bucket with negative thoughts.

If we are depressed, we produce less serotonin. If we are anxious, we produce too many stress hormones which is bad for our health if they are constantly in our blood at high levels.

HOW DO WE PRODUCE SEROTONIN?

A. POSITIVE ACTION

Do the things you like doing: walk the dog, socialise with friends, go to the cinema, listen to music, etc. When you enjoy what you do, you produce a steady flow of serotonin and you will not fill up your stress bucket with negative thoughts.

B. POSITIVE INTERACTION

When you cross the road at a zebra crossing, smile at the drivers who have stopped and put up your hand to say thank you. They repeat the gesture and as a result, you all produce serotonin. It is so easy to smile, say good morning or open a door for someone. It makes us all feel happy and makes the world a better place.

Research shows people who have strong relationships with a partner, family or close friends are happier, healthier and live longer. It works both ways, for us and for them too, so make sure that you make time to spend with your loved ones. In countries where family and friends spend a lot of time together, happiness rates are up, even when they are poorer than the rich western countries.

C. POSITIVE THOUGHTS

We fill up our stress bucket with negative thoughts so we need to think positively. From the moment you realise that you are thinking negatively, you need to stop and pause. Now that you know how the brain works, it is easy to see that your amygdala has kicked in and that your emotional brain is in charge instead of your intellectual brain. The good news is that the pre-frontal cortex, our intellectual boss can overrule the amygdala and take you back to the positive intellectual brain. You just need to say "STOP IT!" and take some deep breaths (high oxygen levels in blood reduce the levels of the stress hormones cortisol and adrenaline). Try out The Swinnen Technique on page 56.

D. OTHER METHODS OF PRODUCING SEROTONIN

- Bright sun light
- Healthy diet with fresh vegetables and oily fish
- Massages
- Laughter

How can you produce more serotonin in your life?

_____

_____

_____

_____

How do we Produce Serotonin?

WHY AM I SELF-DESTRUCTIVE?

THE AMYGDALA, YOUR BODYGUARD, is there to keep you safe. The amygdala is part of your primitive brain and is not capable of intellectual thought. It has to rely on the information in the hippocampus, your filing cabinet. To ensure your survival, the amygdala wants you to repeat actions in the past that did not kill you, and thus are good for you. Unfortunately those actions can kill you in the end, e.g. smoking, drinking, gambling, etc. Only your intellectual brain realises that these habits are bad for you. Unfortunately the amygdala has no idea these actions are slowly killing you.

The annoying little voice in your brain persuading you to have another glass of wine is the amygdala trying to keep you safe. It is very persuasive:

- You had a bad day. Have another glass of wine to make up for it.
- Your day was average. Why not have another glass of wine to make it a fantastic day.
- Your day was excellent. Have another glass of wine to celebrate.

How can we move from the primitive brain to the intellectual brain and switch of that self-destructive voice? Try The Swinnen Technique below and on page 42.

THE SWINNEN TECHNIQUE

1. Imagine what your amygdala looks like.
2. Imagine your amygdala standing on top of your brain.
3. Imagine what your intellectual brain looks like.
4. Imagine your intellectual brain at the bottom of your brain.
5. Take 3 deep breaths.
6. Think of a way in which the intellectual brain can defeat the amygdala and send it back to the bottom of your brain where it belongs. Each time you do this, you will have to imagine a different method (Think of Tom and Jerry. Tom was very creative in finding new ways to catch Jerry.). The intellectual brain can trick the primitive brain somehow, beat him with a baseball bat, use a lasso, etc.
7. Imagine your intellectual brain as the winner, celebrating at the top of your brain.
8. Smile!

Word Search

```
D A N M S I S W I N N E N Y P
E L J A U N M L D S O X T R B
P A H B P T C E O S Z E I H G
R D X J M E B F R S I M Y U E
E G A P A L O F S X I P N N Y
S Y Y W C L C S N T O T I L B
S M F U O E T A I T R L R U H
I A B L P C M V H Y A E C O N
O Y P J P T E A J N I K S R C
N M I V I U L K E A E V J S C
X K A X H A H R G T U X M P O
N T F W M L D M U R E G N A R
O U A U L A T N O R F E R P T
K H S D A Y D R E A M E R U E
N I N O T O R E S O N X H G X
```

Locate these words in the grid, running in one of eight possible directions horizontally, vertically, or diagonally:

- Stress
- Adrenaline
- Cortisol
- Intellectual
- Primitive
- Pre-frontal
- Daydreamer
- Amygdala
- Hippocampus
- Hypothalamus
- Depression
- Anxiety
- Anger
- Swinnen
- Bucket
- REM
- Serotonin

CHAPTER 3
HELPING THE BRAIN

EXERCISE

EXERCISE STIMULATES BRAIN GROWTH

As we get older, the birth of new brain cells slows and our brain tissue shrinks. Exercise may be able to reverse that trend. One brain-scanning study of healthy people who sit down a lot, aged 60 to 79, showed significant increases in brain volume after six months of aerobic fitness training. No such changes occurred among controls that only did stretching and toning exercises. The researchers concluded that the improved cardiovascular fitness that comes with aerobic exercise is associated with fewer age-related changes in the brains of older people. Cardio boosts blood flow to the brain, which delivers much-needed oxygen (the brain soaks up 20 % of all the oxygen in your body).

EXERCISE BOOSTS BRAIN-BUILDING HORMONES

Much like plant food makes plants grow faster and lusher, the chemical known as brain-derived neurotrophic factor, or BDNF, stimulates the growth and proliferation of brain cells. This is especially true in the hippocampus, the brain region that is largely responsible for memory and which is particularly vulnerable to age-related decline. The more you exercise, the more BDNF you produce.

EXERCISE FIGHTS DEPRESSION AND ANXIETY

Depression slows the brain's ability to process information, makes concentration and decision making more difficult, and causes real memory problems. That is because anger and anxiety are opt-out clauses of the primitive brain which is your survival instinct. Exercise helps lift your mood. It cranks up the body's production of serotonin and dopamine, brain chemicals crucial to happy mood. It also boosts levels of the feel-good chemicals called endorphins.

EXERCISE REDUCES THE EFFECTS OF STRESS

If BDNF make the brain younger, other chemicals help age it. These include the stress hormone cortisol. Slow, scattered thinking and forgetfulness are caused by stress more often than we realise. Exercise lowers cortisol levels, helping you to think clearly again. It is also believed to help generate new nerve cells in the brain.

EXERCISE IMPROVES YOUR BRAIN'S EXECUTIVE FUNCTION IN THE PRE-FRONTAL CORTEX

Executive function basically means cognitive abilities like being able to focus on complex tasks, to organise, to think abstractly and to plan for future events. It also aids the working memory, such as the ability to keep a phone number in your head while you dial. When researchers set out to analyse the effects of exercise on executive function, they looked at 18 well-designed studies and found that adults aged 55 to 80 who exercised regularly performed four times better on cognitive tests than control groups who did not exercise.

Workout Planner

MONTLY GOAL _____

	WEEK 1	WEEK 2	WEEK 3	WEEK 4
MONDAY				
TUESDAY				
WEDNESDAY				
THURSDAY				
FRIDAY				
SATURDAY				
SUNDAY				

Workout Planner

MONTLY GOAL _____

	WEEK 1	WEEK 2	WEEK 3	WEEK 4
MONDAY				
TUESDAY				
WEDNESDAY				
THURSDAY				
FRIDAY				
SATURDAY				
SUNDAY				

BRAIN FOODS

The foods you eat play an important role in keeping your brain healthy and can improve specific mental tasks, such as memory and concentration. The following foods boost your brain:

1. WATER

The brain itself is 80 % water. Every chemical reaction that takes place in the brain, including energy production, needs water to occur. This means that water needs to be replenished on a daily basis. The brain is so sensitive to dehydration that even a minimal loss of water can cause symptoms like brain fog, fatigue, dizziness, confusion and more importantly, brain shrinkage.

Next time you feel low, cannot concentrate or have no energy, drink a large glass of water. You will feel better almost immediately.

2. FATTY FISH

This type of fish includes salmon, tuna and sardines, which are all rich sources of omega-3 fatty acids.

Your brain uses omega 3s to build brain and nerve cells. These fats are essential for learning and memory. Omega 3s also have additional benefits for your brain. They may slow age-related mental decline and help ward off Alzheimer's disease. Not getting enough omega 3s is linked to learning impairments, as well as depression.

The British Ministry of Health advises to eat two portions of fish every week, one of which should be oily fish. Omega 3 is also beneficial for a healthy heart, strong bones and beautiful skin.

3. COFFEE

Two main components in coffee, caffeine and antioxidants, help your brain.

The caffeine in coffee has a number of positive effects on the brain, including:

- Increased alertness: caffeine keeps your brain alert by blocking adenosine, a chemical messenger that makes you sleepy.
- Improved mood: caffeine may also boost some of your "feel-good" neurotransmitters, such as serotonin.
- Sharpened concentration: one study found that when participants drank one large coffee in the morning or smaller amounts throughout the day, they were more effective at tasks that required concentration.

Drinking coffee over the long term is also linked to a reduced risk of neurological diseases, such as Parkinson's and Alzheimer's disease. This could at least be partly due to coffee's high concentration of antioxidants.

It is a good idea to drink a glass of water with your coffee as caffeine can dehydrate. Many coffee shops already offer free water.

4. COMPLEX CARBOHYDRATES

Whole grains, brown rice, oats, and sweet potatoes are packed with brain-supportive nutrients such as protein, B vitamins, antioxidants and minerals. They are also a good source of glucose, the main energy source for the brain. Combined with a high-fibre content to stabilise blood sugar levels, these foods support a healthy digestion and therefore boost the immune system too.

Porridge with fruit is a great way to start the day.

5. BLUEBERRIES

Blueberries provide many health benefits, including some that are specifically for your brain. Blueberries and other deeply coloured berries deliver anthocyanins, a group of plant compounds with anti-inflammatory and antioxidant effects.

Antioxidants act against both oxidative stress and inflammation, conditions that may contribute to brain aging and neurodegenerative diseases. Some of the antioxidants in blueberries have been found to accumulate in the brain and help improve communication between brain cells.

6. TURMERIC

This deep-yellow spice is a key ingredient in curry powder and has a number of benefits for the brain. Curcumin, the active ingredient in turmeric, has been shown to cross the blood-brain barrier, meaning it can directly enter the brain and benefit the cells there.

To reap the benefits of curcumin, try cooking with curry powder, adding turmeric to potato dishes to turn them golden or making turmeric tea.

7. BROCCOLI

Broccoli is packed with powerful plant compounds, including antioxidants. It is also very high in vitamin K, delivering more than 100% of the Recommended Daily Intake in a 1-cup serving. This fat-soluble vitamin is essential for forming a type of fat that is densely packed into brain cells. A few studies in older adults have linked a higher vitamin K intake to better memory.

Beyond vitamin K, broccoli contains a number of compounds that give it anti-inflammatory and antioxidant effects, which may help protect the brain against damage.

8. PUMPKIN SEEDS

Pumpkin seeds contain powerful antioxidants that protect the body and brain from free radical damage. They are also an excellent source of magnesium, iron, zinc and copper.

Each of these nutrients is important for brain health.

9. DARK CHOCOLATE

Dark chocolate and cocoa powder are packed with a few brain-boosting compounds, including flavonoids, caffeine and antioxidants.

Flavonoids are a group of antioxidant plant compounds. The flavonoids in chocolate gather in the areas of the brain that deal with learning and memory. Researchers say these compounds may enhance memory and also help slow down age-related mental decline.

10. NUTS

A 2014 review showed that nuts can improve cognition and even help prevent neurodegenerative diseases. Also, another large study found that women who ate nuts regularly over the course of several years had a sharper memory, compared to those who did not eat nuts.

Several nutrients in nuts, such as healthy fats, antioxidants and vitamin E, may explain their brain-health benefits. Vitamin E shields cell membranes from free radical damage, helping slow mental decline.

While all nuts are good for your brain, walnuts may have an extra edge, since they also deliver omega-3 fatty acids.

11. ORANGES

You can get all the vitamin C you need in a day by eating one medium orange. Doing so is important for brain health, since vitamin C is a key factor in preventing mental decline.

Eating sufficient amounts of vitamin C-rich foods can protect against age-related mental decline and Alzheimer's disease. Vitamin C is a powerful antioxidant that helps fight off the free radicals that can damage brain cells. Moreover, vitamin C supports brain health as you age.

You can also get excellent amounts of vitamin C from bell peppers, guava, kiwi, tomatoes and strawberries.

12. EGGS

Eggs are a good source of several nutrients tied to brain health, including vitamins B6 and B12, folate and choline.

Choline is an important micronutrient that your body uses to create acetylcholine, a neurotransmitter that helps regulate mood and memory. Two studies found that higher intakes of choline were linked to better memory and mental function. Nevertheless, many people do not get enough choline in their diet. Eating eggs is an easy way to get choline, given that egg yolks are among the most concentrated sources of this nutrient.

Furthermore, the B vitamins have several roles in brain health. To start, they may help slow the progression of mental decline in the elderly. Also, being deficient in two types of B vitamins, folate and B12, has been linked to depression.

Folate deficiency is common in elderly people with dementia, and studies show that folic acid supplements can help minimise age-related mental decline.

13. GREEN TEA

As is the case with coffee, the caffeine in green tea boosts brain function. In fact, it has been found to improve alertness, performance, memory and focus.

Green tea also has other components that make it a brain-healthy beverage. One of them is L-theanine, an amino acid that can cross the blood-brain barrier and increase the activity of the neurotransmitter GABA, which helps reduce anxiety and makes you feel more relaxed.

L-theanine also increases the frequency of alpha waves in the brain, which helps you relax without making you feel tired. One review found that the L-theanine in green tea can help you relax by counteracting the stimulating effects of caffeine.

It is also rich in polyphenols and antioxidants that may protect the brain from mental decline and reduce the risk of Alzheimer's disease and Parkinson's. Plus, green tea has been found to improve memory.

FOODS TO AVOID:

- Sugary drinks such as lemonade, energy drinks and fruit juice.
- Refined carbohydrates such as white bread and pasta.
- Foods high in trans fats such as hydrogenated vegetable oil used in margarine and ready-made cakes and biscuits.
- Highly processed foods such as chips, sweets, instant noodles, microwave popcorn, ready-made meals and sauces.
- Aspartame which is an artificial sweetener used in many sugar-free products.
- Alcohol which stops the production of serotonin in your brain.
- Fish high in mercury such as shark and swordfish.

Food Planner

	MON	TUE	WED	THUR	FRI	SAT	SUN
B-FAST							
Snack							
LUNCH							
Snack							
DINNER							
Snack							
WATER							
🏃							

Notes:

Food Planner

	MON	TUE	WED	THUR	FRI	SAT	SUN
B-FAST							
Snack							
LUNCH							
Snack							
DINNER							
Snack							
WATER							
🏃							
Notes:							

THE IMPORTANCE OF TOUCH

THE HUMAN TOUCH: A NEGLECTED FEELING

When we are born, the first one of our senses available to us is the sense of touch. Even before we open our eyes, we can already feel physical contact. Experiencing physical contact plays a vital role in our physical and psychological health.

THE EMOTIONAL IMPORTANCE OF OUR SENSE OF TOUCH

Hearing, seeing and smelling are the senses we think of in the context of our own survival. Rarely would we add our sense of touch to that list. Somehow this crucial sense of ours has been underestimated for a long time. This is strange if you think about how useful its function actually is: holding a knife, typing an email on our smartphone, or noticing the heat of a cooker when we put our hand on it (a painful lesson most of us experienced as a child). Our sense of touch is just as important for our survival. Apart from these useful functions, it is responsible for very pleasing sensations as well. How else could we experience the sensation of a touch on our skin, someone holding our hand or kissing us? Not being able to feel those things is hard to imagine and quite dangerous to our well-being as well. Our sense of touch has vital functions for our psychological and physical well-being.

HUGS ARE STRESS BUSTERS

Humans suffer from social isolation but react positively to physical contact. This has to do with the fact that when we hug someone, a hormone called oxytocin is released in our body, which reduces our stress levels. Touch also produces serotonin, the neurotransmitter which determines our general mood. Additionally, our blood pressure lowers and we experience less anxiety during a hug. Nowadays you find hug classes, hug clubs and volunteers handing out hugs in the street.

LONELINESS HAS SEVERE CONSEQUENCES

Our brain and body are thirsty for touch. We are social beings who are only happy if we have other people around us. In an experiment regarding social relations and health, the scientists Louise Hawkley and John Cacioppo collected all related research findings of the past years:

- The risk of suffering from cardiovascular diseases as a young adult is higher in people who were often lonely during childhood and youth.

- A study conducted with retired elderly people showed that loneliness is the most accurate indicator for an individual's lifespan.

- There is a connection between loneliness and depression. If there is positive interaction with other people, we produce serotonin which makes us happy and reduces anxiety and depression.

- Mental abilities deteriorate with increasing loneliness. A study showed that the risk of developing symptoms of Alzheimer's disease is significantly higher with people who feel lonely.

MASSAGES

Now that we know that there is a connection between a lack of physical contact, feeling lonely and depression, what can we do about it? The most obvious answer would be to have more physical contact. But what if you are single or not keen on flinging your arms around a random stranger's neck? The good news is: any kind of physical contact has a pleasing effect on us. If you feel a little short on physical closeness, a simple solution could be to get a massage which also has other health benefits.

PETS

Having a pet is also a good solution. All forms of pleasant physical contact, no matter if from humans or animals, are soothing for our well-being. Pets are cute, warm and like cuddling so they are the ideal partner for getting your daily dose of snuggling if no one else is available.

Cuddle Time!!!

If you do not want the hassle of looking after a pet or you are not allowed a pet, there are many other options: walk a friend's dog, cuddle the neighbour's cat, go horse riding, volunteer at a pet shelter or go to a cat café where there are cats for you to stroke while drinking cappuccino.

THE EFFECT OF MUSIC

Music is an important part of every human culture, both past and present. People around the world respond to music in a universal way. Advances in neuroscience enable researchers to quantitatively measure just how music affects the brain. The interest in the effects of music on the brain has led to a new branch of research called neuromusicology which explores how the nervous system reacts to music. These researchers found that music activates every known part of the brain. Listening to and playing music can make you smarter, happier, healthier and more productive in all stages of life.

MUSIC IMPROVES YOUR MOOD AND REDUCES STRESS

Science has now proven what music lovers already know. Listening to upbeat music can improve your mood. Listening to and playing music reduces chronic stress by lowering the stress hormone cortisol.

One of the ways music affects mood is by stimulating the formation of certain brain chemicals. Listening to music increases the neurotransmitter dopamine. Dopamine is the brain's "motivation molecule" and an integral part of the pleasure-reward system. It is the same brain chemical responsible for the feel-good states obtained from eating chocolate and runner's high. Interestingly, you can further increase dopamine by listening to a playlist that is being shuffled. When one of your favourite songs unexpectedly comes up, it triggers a small dopamine boost.

Playing music with others or enjoying live music stimulates the brain hormone oxytocin.

Oxytocin has been called the "trust molecule" and the "moral molecule" since it helps us bond with and trust others. There is evidence that the oxytocin bump experienced by music lovers can make them more generous and trustworthy.

Music can make you feel more hopeful, powerful, and in control of your life. Listening to sad music has its benefits too. If you are going through a tough time, listening to sad music is cathartic. It can help you get in touch with your emotions to help you heal.

MUSIC MAKES YOU MORE PRODUCTIVE AND CREATIVE

There is strong evidence that listening to music at work can make you a happier, more productive employee. This is especially true if you can choose your own music.

Office workers allowed to listen to their preferred choice of music complete tasks more quickly and come up with better ideas than those who have no control over their musical choices. Background music enhances performance on cognitive tasks, improves accuracy, and enables the completion of repetitive tasks more efficiently.

The effects of music on productivity have been studied in some very specific occupations.

Software developers were happier and produced better work more efficiently when listening to music. When surgeons listened to music while operating, they were less stressed and worked faster and more accurately, especially if they were allowed to pick the music. Music can help people perform better in high-pressure situations. Listening to upbeat music before a game can keep athletes from buckling under pressure.

Music is a source of creativity, especially when it is upbeat. When study participants listened to music labelled "happy," their creativity went up. They came up with more creative solutions and a greater number of ideas than those who listened to other kinds of music or no music at all. Interestingly, participants did not have to like the music they were hearing to reap these benefits.

MUSIC ACTS AS A NATURAL REMEDY

It seems that music can heal whatever is ailing you, be it a mental health disorder or neurological disease.

Music can alleviate the symptoms of mood and mental disorders including:

- Anxiety
- Depression
- Insomnia
- Attention deficit hyperactivity disorder (ADHD)
- Post-traumatic stress disorder (PTSD)
- Schizophrenia

It shows promise in treating stroke, autism, Parkinson's, dementia, and Alzheimer's disease. Music can also help with the psychological aspects of illness and can improve the quality of life in patients with cancer, dementia, Parkinson's and chronic pain. Listening to music reduces the stress experienced by patients both before and after surgery. It can decrease post-operative confusion and delirium that affects some elderly patients while recovering from surgery.

MUSIC AFFECTS EACH BRAIN DIFFERENTLY

One of the most common questions people ask about music is: "What is the best kind of music to listen to?" The answer is: "It depends." Firstly, consider what you hope to achieve.

For example, listening to tunes with lyrics can be distracting if you are trying to learn and process new information. However, this kind of music can actually be helpful if you are working on repetitive or mundane tasks.

A surprising finding is that listening to the wrong kind of music for the situation can sometimes be dangerous! Patients that have undergone heart surgery should not listen to heavy metal music or techno sounds. Doing so can lead to stress and even life-threatening arrhythmias. That is because your body synchronises with the beats and rhythm of the music so this kind of music will get your heart pumping quickly. That is why you should listen to slow music before going to bed so you give your body the opportunity to slow down in tune with the music.

Neuroscientists can now see that music affects each person's brain differently. By using functional magnetic resonance imaging (fMRI), researchers have found that listening to music you like increases blood flow to the brain and brain connectivity more than listening to music you do not like. Also, the number of areas in the brain activated by music varies depending on your musical background and tastes.

Research confirms that the best type of music to increase focus and productivity should first and foremost be music you enjoy. Additionally, it should be instrumental, have an upbeat tempo and be played at medium volume.

WHAT ARE YOUR FAVOURITE SONGS?

MUSIC IS THE MEDICINE OF THE MIND

NATURE

David Strayer, a cognitive psychologist, says that our brains are not tireless machines. They are easily fatigued by our fast-paced, increasingly digital lives. When we slow down and seek out natural surroundings, we not only feel restored but also improve our mental performance.

Strayer has demonstrated as much with a group of participants, who scored 50 % higher on creative problem-solving tasks after three days of wilderness backpacking. If you can have the experience of being in the moment for two or three days, it seems to produce a difference in qualitative thinking because the intellectual brain is in charge. Strayer's hypothesis is that being in nature allows the pre-frontal cortex, our boss, to rest and recover, like an overused muscle.

Researchers from the University of Exeter Medical School in England analysed data from 10,000 city dwellers and found that those living near more green space reported less mental distress, even after adjusting for income, marital status, and employment (all of which are correlated with health).

In 2009, Dutch researchers found a lower incidence of 15 diseases, including depression, anxiety, and migraines, in people who lived within about a half mile of green space. Richard Mitchell, an epidemiologist and a geographer at the University of Glasgow in Scotland, found fewer deaths and less disease in people who lived near green spaces, even if they did not use them. People who have window views of trees and grass have been shown to recover faster in hospitals, perform better in school, and display less violent behaviour.

The National Health Service has allowed doctors in the South West of England to prescribe surfing lessons for teenagers at risk of isolation and mental health problems. They get one-to-one support of a surfing coach.

In some countries, nature is woven into the government's official mental health policy. At the Natural Resources Institute in Finland, the nation's high rates of depression, alcoholism, and suicide led a research team to recommend a minimum nature dose of five hours per month in an effort to improve the nation's mental health. "A 40- to 50-minute walk seems to be enough for physiological changes and mood changes and probably for attention," says Kalevi Korpela, a professor of psychology at the University of Tampere. He has helped design half a dozen "power trails" that encourage mindfulness and reflection.

WHAT LANDSCAPE WOULD YOU LIKE TO WAKE UP TO?

MEDITATION

While there are various types of meditation, the one most commonly talked about involves having a point of focus (your breath, a candle, etc.) and when you become aware that your mind has wandered, returning to your point of focus. The intent is to observe your mind (as opposed to getting lost in it like daydreaming does), raise your awareness of its activity, and learn to not get swept away by thoughts.

Using modern technology like fMRI scans, scientists have developed a more thorough understanding of what is taking place in our brains when we meditate. The overall difference is that our brains stop processing information as actively as they normally would.

HOW MEDITATION AFFECTS YOU

Better Focus

Because meditation is a practice in focusing our attention and being aware of when it drifts, our focus is also improved when we are not meditating. It is a lasting effect that comes from regular sessions of meditation.

Less Anxiety

This point is pretty technical, but it is really interesting. The more we meditate, the less anxiety we have, and it turns out this is because we are actually loosening the connections of particular neural pathways. This sounds bad, but it is not.

Normally the neural pathways from the bodily sensation and fear centres of the brain (the amygdala) to the Default Network Mode (the daydreamer) are really strong. When you experience a scary or upsetting sensation, it triggers a strong reaction, making you feel scared and under attack.

When we meditate, we weaken this neural connection. This means that we do not react as strongly to sensations that might have once lit up our brain. As we weaken this connection, we simultaneously strengthen the connection between the pre-frontal cortex (the boss) and our bodily sensation and fear centres. When we experience scary or upsetting sensations, we can more easily look at them rationally. For example, when you experience pain, rather than becoming anxious and assuming it means something is wrong with you, you can watch the pain rise and fall without becoming stuck in a story about what it might mean. The intellectual brain is at work.

Better Memory

One of the things meditation has been linked to is improving rapid memory recall. Catherine Kerr, a researcher at the Martinos Center for Biomedical Imaging and the Osher Research Center, found that people who practiced mindful meditation were able to adjust the brain wave that screens out distractions and increase their productivity more quickly than those who did not meditate. Kerr said that this ability to ignore distractions could explain "their superior ability to rapidly remember and incorporate new facts."

Less Stress

Mindful meditation has been shown to help people perform under pressure while feeling less stressed. A 2012 study split a group of human resources managers into three, with one third participating in mindful meditation training, another third taking body relaxation training and the last third given no training at all. A stressful multitasking test was given to all the managers before and after the eight-week experiment. In the final test, the group that had participated in the meditation training reported less stress during the test than both of the other groups.

More Grey Matter

Meditation has been linked to larger amounts of grey matter in the hippocampus (your filing cabinet) and the pre-frontal cortex (the boss). More grey matter can lead to more positive emotions, longer-lasting emotional stability, and heightened focus during daily life. Meditation has also been shown to diminish age-related effects on grey matter and reduce the decline of our cognitive functioning.

LAUGHTER

LAUGHTER STRENGTHENS YOUR IMMUNE system, boosts mood, diminishes pain, and protects you from the damaging effects of stress. As children we laugh a lot but as adults, life tends to be more serious and laughter more infrequent. By seeking out more opportunities for humour and laughter, you can improve your emotional health, strengthen your relationships, find greater happiness and even add years to your life:

- Laughter stops distressing emotions. You cannot feel anxious, angry or sad when you are laughing.

- Laughter helps you relax and recharge. It reduces stress hormones and increases energy, enabling you to stay focused and accomplish more.

- Laughter shifts perspective, allowing you to see situations in a more realistic, less threatening light, i.e. you move from your primitive to your intellectual brain. A humorous perspective creates psychological distance, which can help you avoid feeling overwhelmed and diffuse conflict.

- Laughter draws you closer to others and improves relationships, which can have a profound effect on all aspects of your mental and emotional health.

CREATE OPPORTUNITIES TO LAUGH MORE:

- Watch a funny movie, TV series or YouTube video
- Invite friends or colleagues out to a comedy club
- Seek out funny people
- Share a good joke or a funny story
- Check out your bookshop's humour section
- Host a game night with friends
- Play with a pet
- Go to a "laughter yoga" class
- Play with children
- Do something silly
- Make time for fun activities (e.g. bowling, miniature golfing, karaoke)

THE INTERNET

UNFORTUNATELY, WE STILL DO not know the long-term effects of the internet on our brains but scientists have seen some changes already:

THE INTERNET IS OUR EXTERNAL HARD DRIVE

We do not have to remember phone numbers or addresses like we used to. Instead, we can just Google it. According to a study by Science Magazine, "the Internet has become a primary form of external or transactive memory, where information is stored collectively outside ourselves, and our brains have become reliant on the availability of information".

CHILDREN ARE LEARNING DIFFERENTLY

Schools now have computer labs, lap top trolleys and computer corners so children can learn through the internet. There are many educational websites that teach all the school subjects through gaming.

With online libraries, "memorisation is no longer a necessary part of education" according to Read Write Web. Educators are beginning to understand that information is now coming at us quicker and faster than we can digest it, and memorising facts wastes valuable brain power that could be used to keep up with more important information that cannot be quickly Googled.

WE RARELY GIVE TASKS OUR FULL ATTENTION

Have you ever updated your Facebook while listening to music and texting a friend? If so, you have experienced the phenomenon of continuous partial attention and its impact on your brain. It remains to be seen if partial attention is a distraction as most believe, or an adaptation of the brain to the constant flow of stimuli.

WE ARE GETTING BETTER AT FINDING INFORMATION

Although we cannot remember it all, we are getting better at finding the information we need. It seems that the brainpower previously used to retain facts and information is now being used to remember how to look it up. Professor Betsy Sparrow reports, "We remember less through knowing information itself than by knowing where the information can be found." She indicates that this is not necessarily a bad thing as we are adapting to new technology and becoming highly skilled in remembering where to find things.

OUR CONCENTRATION IS SUFFERING

Many teachers and professors are complaining that their students can no longer concentrate for a long spell of time. Our concentration span used to be an average of 50 minutes but for children this has gone down to 15-20 minutes. On top of that, professors also have to deal with students bringing in laptops, tablets and phones that divert their attention.

It is not hard to understand why our concentration span is getting lower. Our time online is often spent scanning headlines and posts and quickly surfing links, never spending much time on any one thing. So of course, when you have to concentrate on information for more than a few minutes, your mind will often begin to wander.

WE ARE BECOMING PHYSICALLY ADDICTED TO TECHNOLOGY

Even after unplugging, many internet users feel a craving for the stimulation received from gadgets. The culprit is dopamine, which is delivered as a response to the stimulation the internet gives you. Without it, you feel bored. After spending time online, your brain wants to get back on for more, making it difficult to concentrate on other tasks and "unplug."

Social media gives our brain the same dopamine hit as alcohol, drugs and gambling. It is very addictive. Unfortunately many of our youngsters are hooked and cannot create normal relationships anymore without the internet.

THE MORE YOU USE THE INTERNET, THE MORE IT LIGHTS UP YOUR BRAIN

In 2007, UCLA professor Gary Small tested experienced surfers and new internet users, asking them to Google a variety of pre-selected topics. In his experiment, he monitored brain activity, noting that experienced surfers showed much more activity than beginner users, especially in the areas typically devoted to decisions and problem solving. He brought them all back six days later, this time having the new users spend an hour each day searching online in the period before they came back. In the second test, the new surfers' brains looked more like the intermediate internet users. "Five hours on the Internet and the naive subjects had already rewired their brains," noted Small, suggesting that over time, internet use changes neural pathways.

WE HAVE BECOME POWER BROWSERS

Online browsing has created a new form of "reading," in which users are not really reading online, but rather power browsing through sites. Instead of left to right, up to down reading, we seem to scan through titles, bullet points, and information that stands out. Comprehension and attention are certainly at risk here.

ONLINE THINKING PERSISTS EVEN OFFLINE

When you are online, you are frequently attacked by bursts of information, which is highly stimulating and even overwhelming. You can become extremely distracted and unfocused with too much information. Even after you log off (if you ever do), your brain remains rewired. A lack of focus and fractured thinking can persist, interrupting work, family, and offline time.

CREATIVE THINKING MAY SUFFER

Some experts believe that memorisation is critical to creativity. William Klemm, a neuroscience professor at Texas A&M University insists that "Creativity comes from a mind that knows, and remembers, a lot." Although creativity seems to have grown with the use of technology, it is certainly being done in new and different ways. Klemm's assertion is certainly true for creative thinking and brainstorming born out of memorised knowledge, which so many of us now store online.

HOW ARE YOU GOING TO SWITCH OFF FROM THE INTERNET:

1.
2.
3.
4.
5.
6.
7.
8.
9.
10.

The Internet

SMOKING

THE NICOTINE IN INHALED tobacco smoke moves from the lungs into the bloodstream and up to a smoker's brain within seven to ten seconds. Once there, nicotine triggers a number of chemical reactions that create temporary feelings of pleasure for the smoker, but these sensations are short-lived, subsiding within minutes.

As the nicotine level drops in the blood, smokers feel edgy and agitated which is the start of nicotine withdrawal. In order to relieve this discomfort, smokers light up another cigarette and so it goes, the vicious cycle of nicotine addiction. One cigarette is never enough, a fact that every smoker knows all too well.

Let us take a look at how nicotine affects brain chemistry:

NICOTINE AND ADRENALIN

When a person inhales cigarette smoke, the nicotine in the smoke is rapidly absorbed into the blood and starts affecting the brain within ten seconds. This causes the release of adrenaline, the "fight or flight" hormone. Physically, adrenaline increases a person's heart rate, blood pressure and restricts blood flow to the heart muscle. When this occurs, smokers experience rapid, shallow breathing and the feeling of a racing heartbeat.

NICOTINE AND INSULIN

Nicotine also inhibits the release of insulin from the pancreas, a hormone that is responsible for removing excess sugar from a person's blood. This leaves the smoker in a slightly hyperglycaemic condition, meaning he or she has more sugar in the blood than is normal.

High blood sugar acts as an appetite suppressant, which may be why smokers experience a reduced feeling of hunger.

NICOTINE AND DOPAMINE

Nicotine activates the same reward pathways in the brain than other drugs of abuse such as cocaine or amphetamines, although to a lesser degree. Research has shown that nicotine increases the level of dopamine in the brain, a neurotransmitter that is responsible for feelings of pleasure and well-being. The acute effects of nicotine wear off within minutes, so smokers must continue to dose themselves up frequently throughout the day to maintain the pleasurable effects of nicotine and to prevent withdrawal symptoms.

THE CHEMICALS IN CIGARETTES

In addition to nicotine, cigarette smoke is composed of more than 7000 toxic chemicals and tar. The tar, which can vary between seven and twenty or more milligrams per cigarette, exposes smokers to an increased risk of lung cancer, emphysema, and bronchial disorders.

Carbon monoxide in cigarette smoke increases the chance of cardiovascular diseases. The Environmental Protection Agency has concluded that second-hand smoke causes lung cancer in both smoking and non-smoking adults and greatly increases the risk of respiratory illnesses in children and sudden infant death syndrome.

QUIT SMOKING NOW

Although stopping smoking can be hard, it is well worth the effort. Your health will benefit almost immediately. Just twenty minutes after your last cigarette, your heart rate slows. Twelve hours later, levels of carbon monoxide, a toxic gas in your blood, return to normal. Your lung function improves and your circulation starts to get better within three months. After a year, your risk of having a heart attack drops by half. And after five to fifteen years, your stroke risk will be the same as that of a non-smoker.

DRUGS

THE BRAIN IS OFTEN compared to an incredibly complex and intricate computer. Instead of electrical circuits on the silicon chips that control our electronic devices, the brain consists of billions of cells, called neurons, which are organised into circuits and networks. Each neuron acts as a switch controlling the flow of information. If a neuron receives enough signals from other neurons connected to it, it "fires", sending its own signal on to other neurons in the circuit.

The brain is made up of many parts with interconnected circuits that all work together as a team. Different brain circuits are responsible for coordinating and performing specific functions. Networks of neurons send signals back and forth to each other and among different parts of the brain, the spinal cord, and nerves in the rest of the body.

To send a message, a neuron releases a neurotransmitter into the gap between it and the next cell. The neurotransmitter crosses the gap and attaches to receptors on the receiving neuron, like a key into a lock. This causes changes in the receiving cell. Other molecules called transporters recycle neurotransmitters (that is, bring them back into the neuron that released them), thereby limiting or shutting off the signal between neurons.

HOW DO DRUGS WORK IN THE BRAIN?

Drugs interfere with the way neurons send, receive, and process signals via neurotransmitters. Some drugs, such as marijuana and heroin, can activate neurons because their chemical structure mimics that of a natural neurotransmitter in the body. This allows the drugs to attach onto and activate the neurons. Although these drugs mimic the brain's own chemicals, they do not activate neurons in the same way as a natural neurotransmitter, and they lead to abnormal messages being sent through the network.

Other drugs, such as amphetamine, speed or cocaine, can cause the neurons to release abnormally large amounts of natural neurotransmitters or prevent the normal recycling of these brain chemicals by interfering with transporters. This too amplifies or disrupts the normal communication between neurons.

HOW DOES DOPAMINE REINFORCE DRUG USE?

Our brains are wired to increase the odds that we will repeat pleasurable activities. The neurotransmitter dopamine is central to this. Whenever the reward circuit is activated by a healthy, pleasurable experience, a burst of dopamine signals that something important is happening that needs to be remembered. This dopamine signal causes changes in neural connectivity that make it easier to repeat the activity again and again without thinking about it, leading to the formation of habits.

Just as drugs produce intense euphoria and pleasure, they also produce much larger surges of dopamine, powerfully reinforcing the connection between consumption of the drug, the resulting pleasure, and all the external cues linked to the experience. Large surges of dopamine "teach" the brain to seek drugs at the expense of other, healthier goals and activities.

Cues in a person's daily routine or environment that have become linked with drug use because of changes to the reward circuit can trigger uncontrollable cravings whenever the person is exposed to these cues, even if the drug itself is not available. This learned "reflex" can last a long time, even in people who have not used drugs in many years. For example, people who have been drug free for a decade can experience cravings when returning to an old neighbourhood or house where they used drugs.

WHY ARE DRUGS MORE ADDICTIVE THAN NATURAL REWARDS?

For the brain, the difference between normal rewards and drug rewards can be compared to the difference between someone whispering into your ear and someone shouting into a microphone. Just as we turn down the volume on a radio that is too loud, the brain of someone who misuses drugs adjusts by producing fewer neurotransmitters in the reward circuit, or by reducing the number of receptors that can receive signals. As a result, the person's ability to experience pleasure from naturally rewarding activities is also reduced.

This is why a person who misuses drugs eventually feels flat, without motivation, lifeless, and/or depressed, and is unable to enjoy things that were previously pleasurable. Now, the person needs to keep taking drugs to experience even a normal level of reward, which only makes the problem worse, like a vicious cycle. Also, the person will often need to take larger amounts of the drug to produce the familiar high.

CHAPTER 4
WHY DO OTHERS STRESS ME OUT?

PERSONALITY TYPES AND THEIR INFLUENCE ON YOUR STRESS BUCKET

If you have ever wondered why some people stress you out, this chapter will explain why. We all have different personalities. Conflicts with other personalities cause negative feelings and fill up your stress bucket which can lead to the primitive brain's three opt-out clauses: depression, anxiety and anger.

INFO

We all display a mixture of different characteristics in different situations with different people. Personality has been studied for hundreds of years and several models are used to help us 'predict' the likelihood of certain behaviours.

Research has shown that analysis of a person's personality cannot predict 'one-off' actions but can give an indication as to the likelihood of behaviours we will show over time.

Our personalities interact with our environment so at any moment in time, we are a product of our personalities and our perceptions. A personality is not learnt. We are born with it and it can be found in the frontal area of our brain.

A commonly used personality model is known as the 'DISC' personality model.

DISC is a personality model based on the work of psychologist William Marston. Marston found that observable behavioural characteristics can be grouped into four major personality types. Each behavioural type tends to exhibit specific characteristics.

DISC itself is purely an acronym for the four personality types which are:

- **Dominance** – which relates to control, power and assertiveness
- **Influence** – which relates to social situations and communication
- **Steadiness** – which relates to patience, persistence, and thoughtfulness
- **Compliance** – which relates to structure and organisation

Everyone possesses all of these personality types but what differs is the extent to which they are more or less one type or another. Essentially a person's 'personality' refers to 'the way they are most often'. Knowing a person's DISC helps you to predict how they might respond to information and how they would like to be dealt with by you.

CHARACTERISTICS OF THE FOUR DISC TYPES

Here is a summary of the four different 'DISC' personality types:

DOMINANCE

People who score high on the D type factors enjoy dealing with problems and challenges. These people will often be described as demanding, forceful, egocentric, strong willed, determined, aggressive, ambitious and pioneering.

High D type people are often found in leadership positions. This does not mean they are good leaders as their weaknesses often include being poor listeners, being impatient and insensitive to others.

D type people are bottom-line people who hate to waste time. They want straight talk and direct answers to their "WHAT" questions.

Status is very important to D type people so they will buy expensive watches, clothes and cars. They join expensive clubs.

High D type people are prone to anger as their primitive brain's opt out clause.

INFLUENCE

People who score high on the I type factors influence others through talking and activity. They tend to be emotional. They are commonly described as enthusiastic, magnetic, persuasive, warm, trusting, demonstrative and optimistic.

They like people and thrive in a social scene. It is important that others have a favourable impression of them. Indeed high I people are more interested in people than in accomplishing tasks. Time does tend to get away from them and everything takes a lower priority when they are discussing ideas. They believe everything will be all right and everyone is "such a nice person". They are excellent at communication, marketing and sales.

They need freedom of expression. They can become easily distracted as they have trouble staying focused. They tend to think in the future. They want answers to their "WHO" questions.

High I people can be very dramatic and move from depression to anxiety, anger and happiness at a fast rate.

STEADINESS

High S people do not like sudden change. They like a steady pace and security. These people are calm, relaxed, patient, predictable, deliberate, stable, consistent and can tend to be unemotional and poker faced.

Steady people get along well with others because they are flexible in their attitude. They may not say anything if they disagree because they like to keep the peace. They like to help others and make good counsellors as they are great listeners. They make good doctors, nurses and teachers.

Steady people like to maintain familiar and predictable patterns. If they receive appreciation, they maintain a high level of performance. They do a lot of the hard work in the background and are not often noticed. They like to feel comfortable with anything new before actually starting it.

Steady people will want answers to their "HOW" and "WHEN" questions.

High S type people are prone to depression as their primitive brain's opt out clause.

COMPLIANCE

People who score high on the C type adhere to rules, regulations and structure. They like to do things well and do them well first time. They are slow paced and task oriented.

High C people are commonly described as careful, cautious, neat, systematic and accurate. Perfection is very important to C people, and they tend to be critical of themselves. They will study privately to learn about a subject before discussing it in public. They like technical jobs, e.g. engineering, auditing, accounting, etc.

People can find it difficult to read high C people as they do not show their feelings. They tend to protect their privacy. They make to-do lists. Compliant people want answers to their "WHY" and "HOW" questions.

High C type people are prone to anxiety as their primitive brain's opt out clause.

IDENTIFYING DISC PERSONALITIES

If you are just getting to know someone and have not had time to observe many of their behavioural characteristics then here are a few tips to help:

- D people: Dominance
- I people: Influence
- S people: Steadiness
- C people: Compliance

D and I people are fast-paced. They will speak quickly and fill in forms quickly. S and C people will talk slower, and take their time to fill in any forms. C people in particular will be meticulous when filling out any form. They will have very neat handwriting, whereas I people will likely have a big, loopy messy scrawl.

S and I people are people focused and more likely to be chatty. As S type people are team oriented and like to help others, expect them to ask questions about you and talk about and praise others, while the I type person will love to chat about themselves and get the gossip on who is doing what, and to whom.

D and C people are task focused, so they will not be too chatty. In fact, you may feel that trying to get any personal information from them is like pulling teeth. C people will ask lots of questions about anything whereas D people will just want to get on with it. D people will likely be up close and personal and hold direct eye contact with you whereas C people will appear to be less confident or direct with their body language.

YOUR ONLINE DISC PERSONALITY TEST

IT IS VERY USEFUL to know what DISC personality mix you are. It helps you to understand yourself and why other personalities might be stressing you out.

You can probably already guess what your personality mix is but to be sure; go to the following URL (*https://www.123test.com/disc-personality-test/*) to do an online DISC personality test. The test will take about ten minutes and you will see your results immediately. This is an example of some of the information it will give you.

Your Online DISC Personality Test

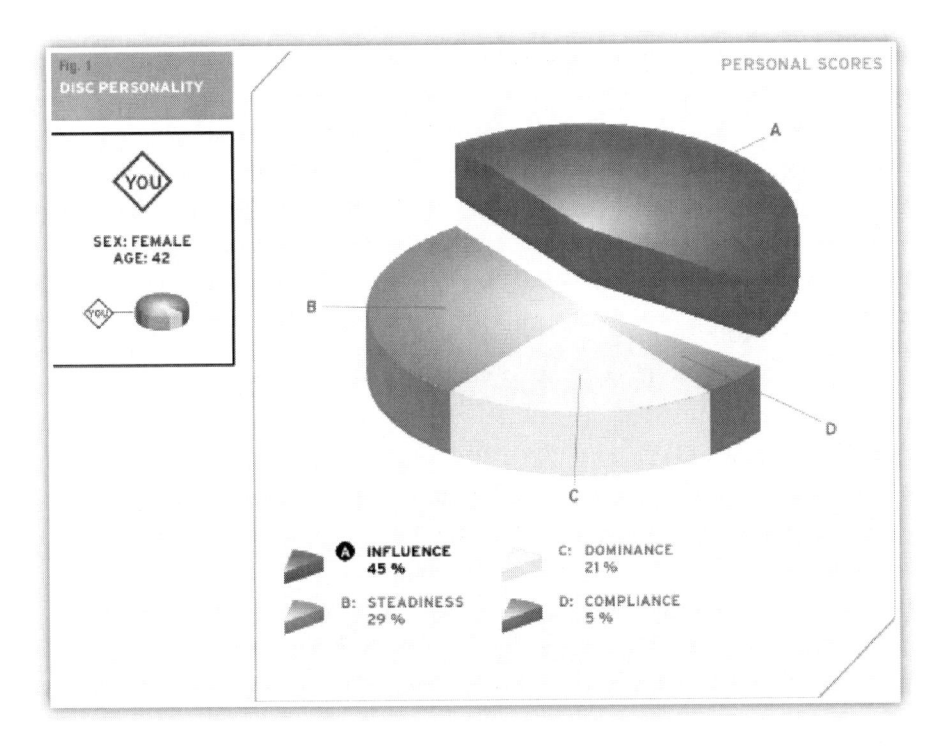

Fig. 1
DISC PERSONALITY

PERSONAL SCORES

SEX: FEMALE
AGE: 42

- A: **INFLUENCE** 45 %
- B: STEADINESS 29 %
- C: DOMINANCE 21 %
- D: COMPLIANCE 5 %

Your DISC personality type

Your unique sequence of scores characterizes you in a specific way. The positive impact you are likely to make on people is:

- You are an approachable and understanding person.
- Your optimism encourages you to look for the best in others.
- You are likely to be a good listener and offer constructive advice rather than imposing your own ideas and values on others.
- Developing and maintaining relationships - at work and at play is important to you.

ADAPTING YOUR BEHAVIOUR TO INFLUENCE OTHERS

DIFFERENT PERSONALITY STYLES CAN clash and fill up your stress bucket! A D style person who may appear aggressive and insensitive to others is likely to annoy a S style person who is likely to be very sensitive to the needs of others. A fast-talking scatter-brained I type person is likely to annoy a slow thinking C type perfectionist, and vice versa.

This is why it is important for you to know and understand your own DISC, so that you do not inadvertently clash with others. It also highlights to you where you will need to adapt your typical behaviour to ensure you interact effectively and positively with everyone, all of the time. Here are some guidelines for successful interaction:

DOMINANT PERSONALITY

- Show them how they can succeed!
- Show them how they can fail!
- Build respect to avoid conflict.
- Focus on facts and ideas rather than people as they are self-centred.
- Have evidence to support your ideas and advice.
- Be quick, focused and get to the point.
- Ask 'what' not 'how'.

INFLUENTIAL PERSONALITY

- Be sociable and friendly with them.
- Listen to them and talk about their ideas.
- Help them find ways to translate the talk into useful action.
- Do not spend too much time on the details.
- Motivate them to follow through to complete tasks.
- Recognise their accomplishments. They love parties!

STEADY PERSONALITY

- Be genuinely interested in them.
- Recognise and appreciate their achievements.
- Create a human working environment for them.
- Give them time to adjust to change.
- Clearly define goals for them and provide ongoing support.
- Avoid hurry and pressure.
- Present new ideas carefully.

COMPLIANT PERSONALITY

- Warn them before and generally avoid surprises.
- Be well prepared. Do not be spontaneous with them if you can help it.
- Be logical, accurate and use clear data.
- Show how things fit into the bigger picture.
- Be specific in disagreement and focus on the facts.
- Be patient, persistent and diplomatic as they are not good with people and communication.

EXAMPLE

Someone in your office has parked their car like this:

You know whose car this is and their DISC personality. You need them to move their car. What should you say to them?

Dominant Personality

Tips: D people like status. This is not a typical car for a D person so it must be the spouse's or the maid's. They are proud of their parking and traffic fines.

What you say:

_____

_____

_____

_____

Influential Personality

Tips: I people are friendly and like chit chat. They probably did not notice they parked in two spaces because they were waving at someone or singing a song. I people need to be pushed into action.

What you say:

_____

_____

_____

_____

_____

Steady Personality

Tips: S people are people-oriented and are the helpers of the world so it is unlikely they would park like this.

What you say:

_____

_____

_____

_____

_____

Compliant personality

Tip: This situation is not possible for C people as they measure the parking space to make sure they are in the centre.

What you say:

Here are some suggestions on how to influence the different personalities.

SUGGESTIONS

Dominant Personality:

"Hi, I saw your nice car in the car park. I would not park it like that because if a woman tries to park next to it, she might scratch or damage it."

Influential Personality:

"Hi, good morning. How are you? How was your weekend? (Wait for the reply)

I saw your car outside. Did you know it was parked in the middle of two spaces? (wait for the shock of surprise and apologies).

Would you mind moving your car so others can get in please?"

(The I person will agree immediately and tell a story of a time that happened before. To push them into action, ask where their keys are and suggest you walk and talk at the same time. Walk to the car park with them while chatting and make sure they move the car).

Steady Personality:

"Hi, good morning. How are you? I saw your car outside. Did you know it was parked in the middle of two spaces? Would you mind moving it so others can park there please? People with wheelchairs and buggies need more space."

(The S person will be very embarrassed, apologise many times and move the car immediately).

Compliant Personality:

Compliant people would rather die than park in two spaces.

CHAPTER 5

HOW DO I SOLVE MY PROBLEMS?

STAGES OF PROBLEM SOLVING

EFFECTIVE PROBLEM SOLVING USUALLY involves working through a number of steps or stages, such as those outlined below.

1. PROBLEM IDENTIFICATION

It might well be that your amygdala is in overdrive and that you are functioning in your primitive mind. That is why you can see so many threats and problems. If this is the case, we need to get you back to the intellectual brain. How can you do this? Use The Swinnen Technique explained on page 42.

It could well be that the problem has already gone away, just by thinking clearly. If not, it might still go away by itself. The saying "sleep on it" is a very useful one. Dreaming will give a conclusion to unfinished emotions and concerns and the third and fourth phase of your sleep will heal the body so there might be no need to book an appointment with the doctor after you had a good night's sleep.

If you decide there is still a problem and you can define it, you go to the next stage.

2. STRUCTURING THE PROBLEM

In this stage you need to think about why there is a problem. Do you have toxic people in your life? Do you eat too much because you miss your family? Is your boss stressing you out?

If the problem is complex, you might want to write down all the information you can find, e.g. why is my company making a loss?

It might help to talk to others as they might have another view of the problem. The more information you find, the better the solution.

3. LOOKING FOR POSSIBLE SOLUTIONS

This is the stage where you look for possible solutions. Again, it is worth involving different people and doing some brain-storming. Ideally, ask a lot of people and different personality types because they each solve problems in a different way.

Do not evaluate the ideas yet, even if they sound completely crazy. You do that in the next stage.

4. MAKING A DECISION

Have a look at the possible solutions and evaluate them. Are they possible? They might be too expensive, too complicated, take too long or be illegal. Take a piece of paper and write your problem and solution at the top, e.g. "Should I replace my old car with a new one?" Then, you draw 2 columns: "Yes" and "No". In each column you are going to write the reasons why. You can even involve your feelings. When you have completed these, you can score them points out of 10. The winning score gives you the right decision.

Example:

SHOULD I REPLACE MY OLD CAR WITH A NEW ONE?				
Yes	**Score**	**No**	**Score**
Better comfort	7/10	Cost means no holiday	10/10
Lower fuel costs	6/10	Higher insurance	7/10
Lower servicing costs	8/10	Time and hassle to find it	4/10
Better for family use	6/10	Disposal or sale of old car	4/10
Better reliability	10/10	Big decisions like this scare me	5/10
It will be load of mind	4/10		
I will look cool	7/10		
Total	**48**	**Total**	**30**
YOU HAVE DECIDED TO BUY A NEW CAR.			

5. IMPLEMENTATION

Implement the solution you have chosen. If you have gone through stages 1 - 4 well, it will be a good solution to your problem.

6. MONITORING/SEEKING FEEDBACK

This stage is often forgotten. After a certain period, e.g. a week or month, you look at your implemented solution again to see if the problem has gone away. It might be worth talking to others to see if they agree. If all is well, celebrate! You deserve it. If the solution needs tweaking, you can go through the problem solving stages again.

CHAPTER 6
WHY CAN'T I CHANGE?

THE ADKAR TECHNIQUE

We all want to be happier and healthier. Even when we try very hard, it is difficult to change and that is why many of us have problems with stopping smoking or drinking, losing weight and becoming fit.

Prosci developed a model called ADKAR which tells you why you can't change and how you can help yourself and others to change.

ADKAR stands for:

Awareness

Desire

Knowledge

Ability

Reinforcement

AWARENESS

The first thing you need to do is check if people are aware of the change that needs to be made. This sounds silly but it is the main cause why people have not made the change. They did not know about the change or why they have to change. It might well be that they missed an informative email or meeting about a new rule, a new system or procedure.

Solution: Check if people are aware of the change and why it needs to happen. If needed, give them the information and people will make the change.

DESIRE

This is the most difficult cause to deal with. Smokers and obese people know that smoking and being overweight is unhealthy and might kill them. If they do not want to change, they won't. You have probably heard a smoker say: "I have to die of something. It might as well be smoking" or "I have the right to smoke." Smokers give up when they are ready to change. This could be because they are in love, have babies or had a health scare.

Solution: The carrot and stick technique. How do you make a donkey walk? By holding a carrot in front of its nose or hit it with a stick. If the person changes, celebrate and if the person does not, implement consequences.

KNOWLEDGE

The person might know about the change and wants to change, but do they know how to change? Let us say that your boss wants you to do a Prezi presentation instead of a PowerPoint presentation. You want to help your boss but you have no idea how to create a Prezi presentation.

Solution: Training courses are the perfect way of to pass on knowledge.

ABILITY

Are people able to change? Their environment plays a big role in this. Smokers find it difficult to stop because they will not be able to join their smoker friends at breaks. They will be losing out on that camaraderie. Where do you socialize with friends? You usually meet at pubs, coffee shops and restaurants and eating and drinking is involved. A take-away at a friend's house is another popular option. No wonder that we put on weight if you count the calories of socialising.

Solution: Tell your friends about the change you want to push through and ask them to help you. You need coaches and mentors to help you. Why not walk to the coffee bar instead of driving? AA (Alcoholics Anonymous) has an excellent "buddy system". Each member gets a buddy that will help them if they want to start drinking again. It is an example of how others can coach and mentor you effectively.

REINFORCEMENT

Some people who stopped smoking for years start again and we all know the concept of yo yo dieting where people put all the weight back on (and more) that they previously lost. If this is the case, you need to bring in reinforcement.

Solution: Reinforcement is a regular check-up, ideally by a professional or mentor. Doctors have check-ups to kick-start their patients' healthy life style. They complement good behaviour and remind them of the consequences of unhealthy choices. Your doctor's surgery offers a lot of classes and support, e.g. for depression, anxiety and anger management, quitting smoking and drinking, losing weight, etc.

EXERCISE: WHY CAN'T YOU CHANGE?

Briefly describe the personal change you are trying to implement and score yourself 1 to 5. (1 is low and 5 is high)

1. AWARENESS:

Do you know about the change and why the change is necessary?

Score: /5

2. DESIRE:

Do you want to change?

Score: /5

3. KNOWLEDGE:

Do you know how to change?

Score: /5

Exercise: Why Can't You Change?

4 ABILITY:

Are you able to change?

Score: /5

5. REINFORCEMENT:

Do you have regular check-ups and reinforcement in place so you stick to the change?

Score: /5

Now look at the next page for your score interpretation.

SCORE INTERPRETATION

Now consider the first area in which your score was three or below. You must address this area before anything else is done. For example, if you identified awareness as the area with a low score, then working on desire, knowledge or skill development will not help you make the change happen.

On the other hand, if you identified desire, then continually repeating your reasons for change is useless because you know these reasons. You must address your desire to change. Desire may stem from negative or positive consequences. The consequences have to be great enough to overcome your personal threshold to resist change.

If knowledge was the area you identified, then you want to be careful not to dwell on the reasons for change and the motivating factors. What is required is education and training for the skills and behaviours that are needed for change.

If ability was the area selected with the low score, then several steps are required to move forward. You will need time to develop new skills and behaviours. Just like learning a new sport or any new skill, time is required to develop new abilities. You will need ongoing coaching and support. No one-time training event or educational program will substitute for ongoing coaching and mentoring.

Finally, if reinforcement was the area identified, then you will need to investigate if the necessary elements are present to keep you from reverting to old behaviours. Address the incentives or consequences for not continuing to act in the new way.

CHAPTER 7
DEALING WITH BIG CHANGES AND LOSS

KUBLER-ROSS CHANGE CURVE

It is useful to know the different emotions individuals go through when faced with big changes and loss as they also **involve depression, anxiety and anger.**

Initially Elisabeth Kubler-Ross published her seminal work on 'Death and Dying' in 1969, describing her work with terminally ill patients and the psychological stages they go through when coming to terms with their condition. It has been recognised that individuals go through these stages when faced with any big change or loss, e.g. changes at work, redundancy, divorce, illness, etc.

Different people move through the stages at different speeds and there may be some overlap between the stages. It is important to recognise this. The individual's history, personality type, the type of change and the consequence of change are also key factors in how an individual is going to respond to change and move through the stages in different situations.

Kubler-Ross Curve Applied To Business Change

DENIAL
«They aren't really going to go through with it»

ANGER
«What a waste of time and money. How much do those stupid consultants cost?»

BARGAINING
«If they want me to do that, fine but I wont have time to get on with my other duties,
Or
If they make me do that I'll resign»

Depression
«This really is happening and there is nothing I can do about it»

Acceptance
«Well, this is how it is, but things aren't so bad»

Moving On
«Actually this new set up is better than the old and I can see how I can make this work for me»

Motivation/Performance

HOW CAN WE HELP PEOPLE THROUGH THE STAGES?

SHOCK OR DENIAL

"I can't believe it",
"This can't be happening",
"Not to me!", "Not again!"

Denial is usually a temporary defence technique that gives us time to absorb news of change before moving on to other stages. It is the initial stage of numbness and shock. We do not want to believe that the change is happening. If we can pretend that the change is not happening, if we keep it at a distance, then maybe it will all go away. This is a bit like an ostrich burying its head in the sand.

Start communicating that there is a problem early on. Do not withhold information that indicates that things are not going so well. Give them all the information. This will minimise the shock or denial phase as people will have begun to see that there is a need for change, even if they are unaware of the form that it will take.

Do not try and sell them on the idea that things are better for them yet. They are not ready to hear this.

Unfortunately, there are many unscrupulous people making a lot of money out of the denial stage of others. If you Google "cure for cancer", thousands of websites will offer to sell you pills, sprays, food, drinks, water, retreats, etc. that will miraculously cure your illness.

ANGER

"Why me? It's not fair!"
"NO! I can't accept this!"

When we realise that the change is real and will affect us, our denial usually turns to anger. Now we get angry and look to blame someone or something else for making this happen to us. Our anger can be directed in many different directions: the boss, the economic crisis, senior management, Brexit, etc.

Practise patience and empathy and do not try to suppress conflict. Provide a verbal outlet for people to show their anger. Once they get their grievances and anger out in the open, bitterness and frustration can be reduced.

Although people will be angry, that does not mean that what they say has no value. They may have legitimate concerns so still listen to them and pay attention to holes they may be pointing out in the plan.

Remember that people are not attacking you personally (although that is not always the case); remain calm and patient.

BARGAINING

"Just let me work to see my children graduate.";
"I'll do anything if you give me more time. A few more years?"

We start bargaining in order to put off the change or find a way out of the situation. In a work situation someone might work harder and put in lots of overtime to prove themselves invaluable in order to avoid losing their job.

When people start trying to bargain, depending on the nature of it, ask them to give the change a chance. A lot of bargaining is done while people are still angry. Once the anger disappears, then so does much of the bargaining people were trying to do.

DEPRESSION

"I'm so sad, why bother with anything?";
"What's the point of trying?"

When we realise that bargaining is not going to work, the reality of the change sets in. At this point we become aware of the losses associated with the change and what we have to leave behind. This has the potential to move people towards a sad state, feeling down and depressed with low energy. They might take sick leave or mental health days.

Be patient and supportive. Listen to them and stay positive. Inform them of all the positive options there are for them and encourage them to act on them.

ACCEPTANCE

"It's going to be OK.";
"I may as well prepare for it."

Acceptance is not a happy space, but rather a resigned attitude towards the change, and a sense that they must get on with it. For the first time people start considering their options. It is a bit like a train heading into a tunnel: "I don't know what's in there, I have to keep going on this track, I'm scared but have no option, I hope there's light at the end." This can be a creative space as it forces people to explore and look for new possibilities.

Help people acknowledge it is the end of an era, support them in their new roles and encourage them to take responsibility. Set goals with them of which they can take ownership.

Begin to stress the benefits of the new situation and how it can work for the individual.

Plan for some early successes for the change initiative and then communicate them loudly. Once people can see that it is working then they will be less sceptical and more positive about the change.

MOVING ON

"I can do this!"

Help people to take the ball and run with it. Let them find ways of using the new set up to create and stretch goals and encourage them to push performance. Let people innovate and take risks within the new set up: let them not only see ways of making the new system work in their favour but put those into practice. When people do really well, reward them.

How can we Help People Through the Stages?

WORD PUZZLE

```
N M I A Q O I H P G Z B E T E
O O N B I S P F F M A C N N G
I N F I C E Y T W R N E O H D
T I L L F O J W G A M I W Z E
A T U I W M M A T E T R D R L
T O E T X A I P C U E E G A W
N R N Y Y N E R L G S B K K O
E I C B I C O O N I X H U D N
M N E N C F S A R V A D F A K
E G G A N S T E A D I N E S S
L I R I P D O M I N A N C E F
P P E N O I S S E R P E D E I
M R D I S C S S E N E R A W A
I L A I N E D I P R O B L E M
C Z J Z Y A P M E I T V W O P
```

Locate these words in the grid, running in one of eight possible directions horizontally, vertically, or diagonally:

- DISC
- Dominance
- Influence
- Steadiness
- Compliance
- Problem
- Solution
- Implementation
- Monitoring
- ADKAR
- Awareness
- Desire
- Knowledge
- Ability
- Reinforcement
- Denial
- Anger
- Bargaining
- Depression
- Acceptance

CHAPTER 8
SELF HELP PLANNER

HOW TO USE THE SELF HELP PLANNER

THERE IS ONE PAGE for each week. Pick a day in the week that you would like to use your planner and try and stick to that day. You can do this by yourself or with a friend, spouse, parent, etc. If you prefer to work with one of our stress management coaches, just send an email to *info@becsltd.com*. We can help.

First of all, think of all the positive things you experienced in the last seven days and write them down. Have you gone out with friends? Walked the dog? Watched a movie with friends? Gone swimming? Lost weight?

Secondly, how do you feel now? Give yourself a score between 0 (very unhappy) and 10 (very happy).

What concrete steps can you take in the next seven days for you to score higher in a week's time? Give a lot of detail. "Getting fit" is too vague. How will you get fit? Will you go to the gym? When? What time? Where? How? Who with?

The more detailed your goal of the week, the better!

Listen to the relaxation recording on the last page. It will help you make good decisions and increase your self-confidence.

Enjoy your journey!

Goals for Your Mind, Body & Soul

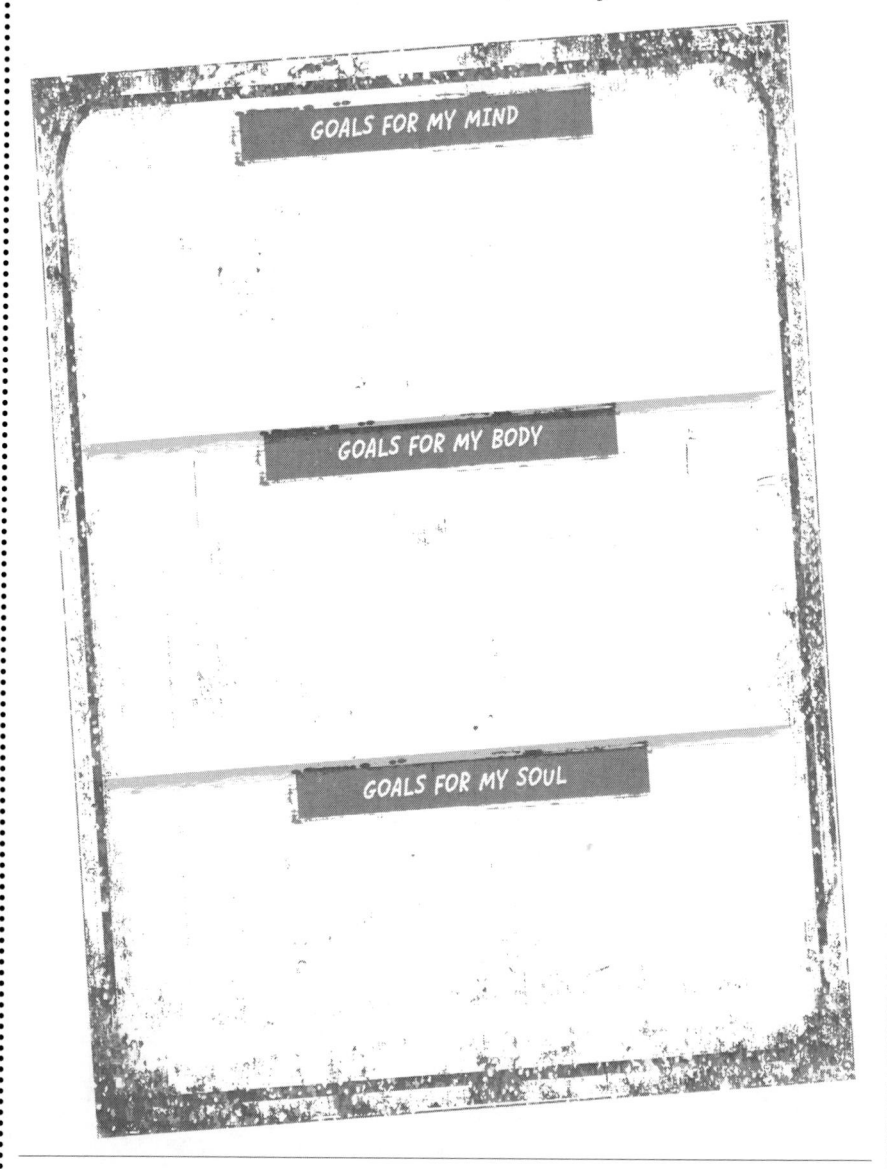

GOALS FOR MY MIND

GOALS FOR MY BODY

GOALS FOR MY SOUL

WEEK 1

What positive things have you experienced in the last seven days?

-
-
-
-
-
-
-

How do you feel? Give yourself a score: **/10**

What is your goal for this week? Give a lot of details: what, where, when, what time, how, who with?

-
-
-
-
-
-
-

PUZZLE

1. St__ss is n_t _lwa_s b_d.

2. The _ntel___tu_l b__in is p_s_t_ve.

3. The p_e_fr_nt_l c_rt_x is t_e b_ss.

4. The p_e_fro_t_l cor_ex w_n_s to _ch_ev_ your g_a_s.

5. Da_dre_m_ng is g_o_ f_r us.

6. Th_ pr_mit_ve br_in is n_g_tiv_.

7. Th_ pr_mit_ve bra_n ke_ps y_u _l_ve.

8. T_e _mygd_l_ is yo_r _od_gu_rd.

9. The h_pp_ca_p_s is y_ur f_li_g _ab_n_t.

10. The h_poth_lam_s is y_ur ch_m_st.

Answers on page 185.

WEEK 2

What positive things have you experienced in the last seven days?

- _____
- _____
- _____
- _____
- _____
- _____
- _____

How do you feel? Give yourself a score: [ ] /10

What is your goal for this week? Give a lot of details: what, where, when, what time, how, who with?

- _____
- _____
- _____
- _____
- _____
- _____
- _____

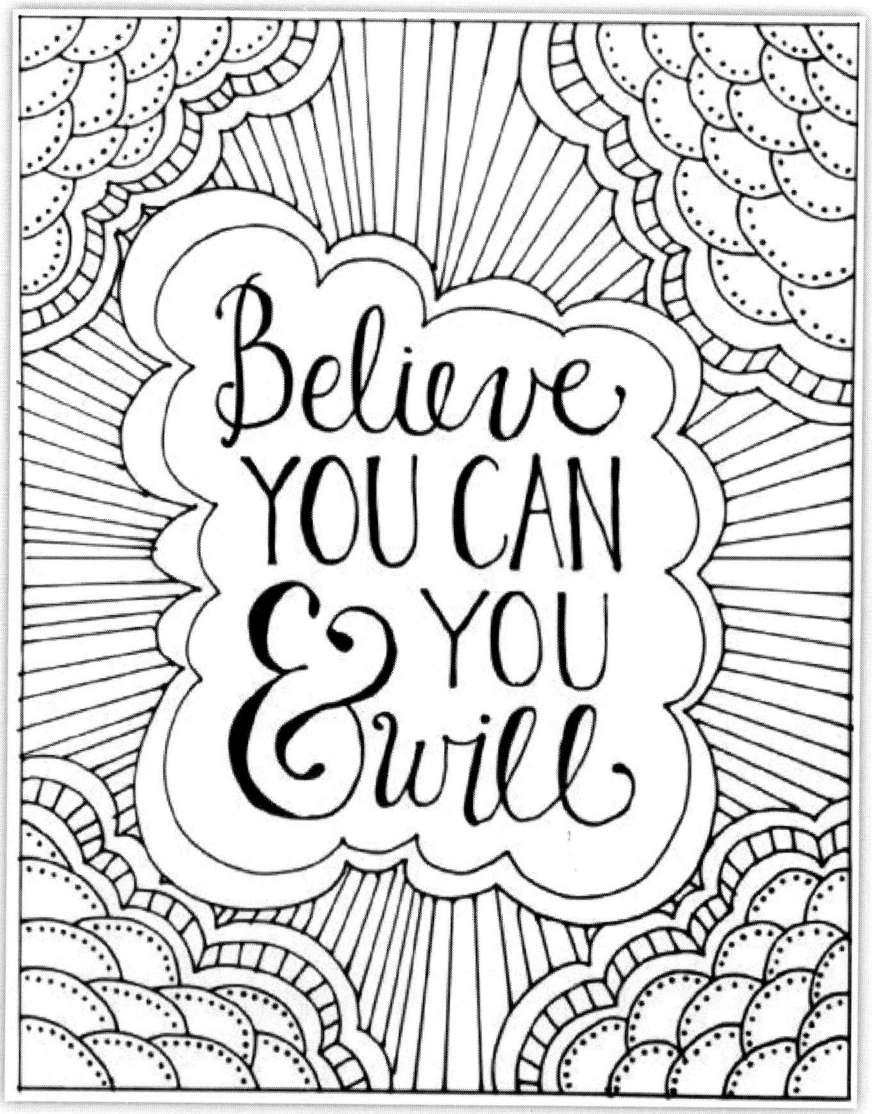
Believe
YOU CAN
& YOU
will

WEEK 3

What positive things have you experienced in the last seven days?

- _____
- _____
- _____
- _____
- _____
- _____
- _____

How do you feel? Give yourself a score: ☐ /10

What is your goal for this week? Give a lot of details: what, where, when, what time, how, who with?

- _____
- _____
- _____
- _____
- _____
- _____
- _____

QUIZ 1: TRUE OR FALSE

1. Depression, anxiety and anger are all opt out clauses of the primitive brain. ☑ ☒

2. When your stress bucket overflows you find it difficult to cope. ☑ ☒

3. REM sleep empties your stress bucket. ☑ ☒

4. Sleep heals your body. ☑ ☒

5. A good night's sleep stops you from overeating the next day. ☑ ☒

6. You dream about what will happen in the future. ☑ ☒

7. When you produce plenty of serotonin, you will be in a good mood. ☑ ☒

8. You have to be involved in a charity to produce serotonin. ☑ ☒

9. Alcohol stops the production of serotonin. ☑ ☒

10. Smoking halves the production of serotonin. ☑ ☒

Answers on page 185.

WEEK 4

What positive things have you experienced in the last seven days?

-
-
-
-
-
-
-

How do you feel? Give yourself a score: ☐ **/10**

What is your goal for this week? Give a lot of details: what, where, when, what time, how, who with?

-
-
-
-
-
-
-

HOW FULL IS YOUR STRESS BUCKET?

HOW CAN YOU EMPTY IT?

WEEK 5

What positive things have you experienced in the last seven days?

-
-
-
-
-
-
-

How do you feel? Give yourself a score: ___/10

What is your goal for this week? Give a lot of details: what, where, when, what time, how, who with?

-
-
-
-
-
-
-

QUIZ 2: TRUE OR FALSE

1. Exercise fights depression and anxiety. ☐✓ ☐✗

2. Exercise produces serotonin, dopamine and endorphins. ☐✓ ☐✗

3. Exercise increases your brain volume, even when you are over 70 years old. ☐✓ ☐✗

4. Coffee is bad for your brain. ☐✓ ☐✗

5. Hugs are good for your health. ☐✓ ☐✗

6. Loneliness does not impact on your health. ☐✓ ☐✗

7. Music improves your mood and reduces stress. ☐✓ ☐✗

8. Patients who have window views of trees and grass recover faster in hospital. ☐✓ ☐✗

9. You are healthier and happier if you live near a park, even when you never walk in it. ☐✓ ☐✗

10. Meditation has no effect on your memory. ☐✓ ☐✗

Answers on page 185.

WEEK 6

What positive things have you experienced in the last seven days?

-
-
-
-
-
-
-

How do you feel? Give yourself a score: __/10

What is your goal for this week? Give a lot of details: what, where, when, what time, how, who with?

-
-
-
-
-
-
-

WHAT IS YOUR DISC PERSONALITY?

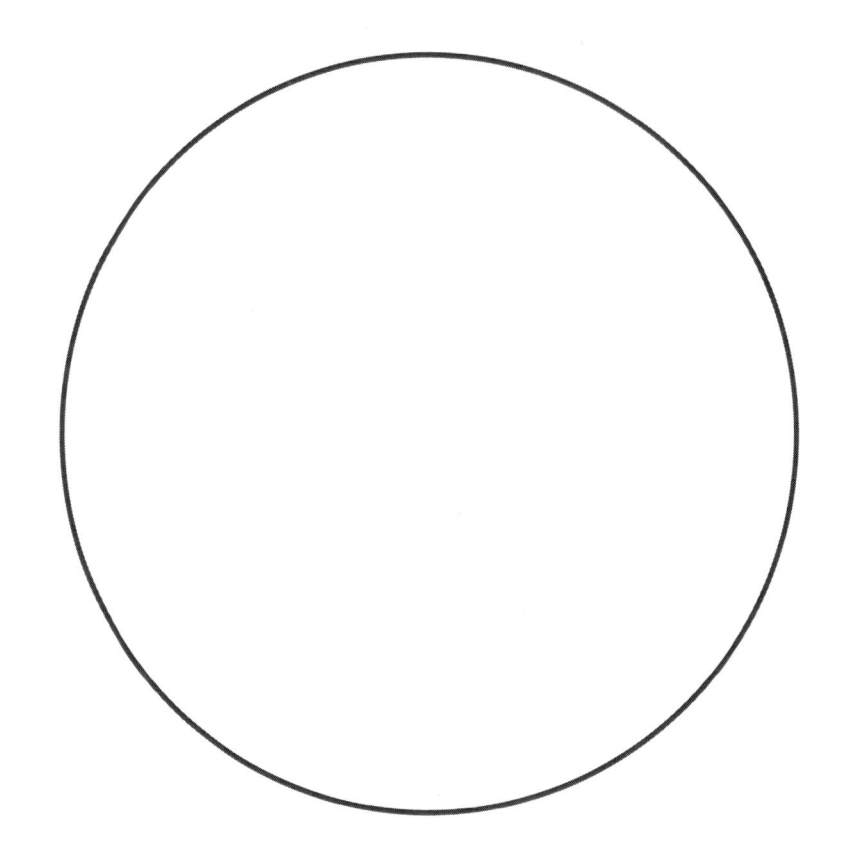

My DISC personality is a mix of:

- % dominance
- % influence
- % steadiness
- % compliance

Draw your mix in the circle graph and colour in:

- Dominance: red
- Influence: yellow
- Steadiness: green
- Compliance: blue

WEEK 7

What positive things have you experienced in the last seven days?

-
-
-
-
-
-
-

How do you feel? Give yourself a score: /10

What is your goal for this week? Give a lot of details: what, where, when, what time, how, who with?

-
-
-
-
-
-
-

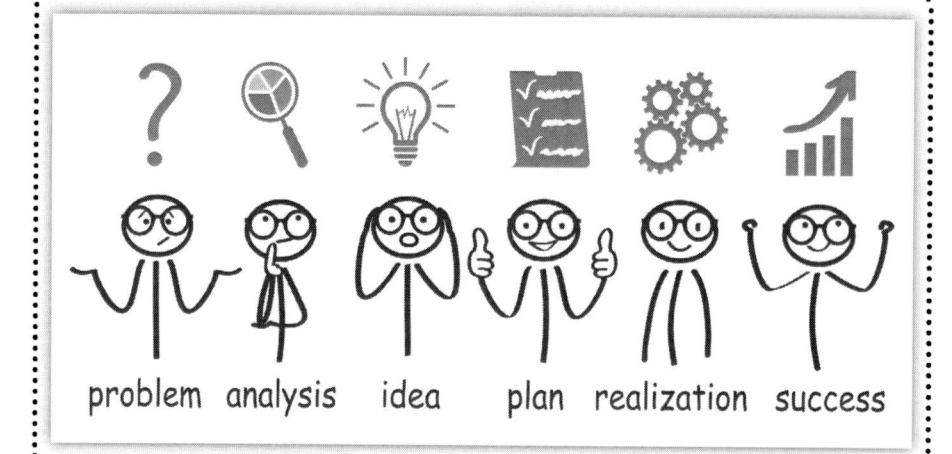

problem   analysis   idea   plan   realization   success

ANY PROBLEMS?

Try using the steps above to solve them.

WEEK 8

What positive things have you experienced in the last seven days?

-
-
-
-
-
-
-

How do you feel? Give yourself a score: /10

What is your goal for this week? Give a lot of details: what, where, when, what time, how, who with?

-
-
-
-
-
-
-

WOULD YOU LIKE TO CHANGE?

Make it real and draw your perfect life.

WEEK 9

What positive things have you experienced in the last seven days?

- _____
- _____
- _____
- _____
- _____
- _____
- _____

How do you feel? Give yourself a score: ☐ /10

What is your goal for this week? Give a lot of details: what, where, when, what time, how, who with?

- _____
- _____
- _____
- _____
- _____
- _____
- _____

SUFFERED A BIG CHANGE OR LOSS?

Where are you on the graph now?

Where would you like to be?

How will you get there?

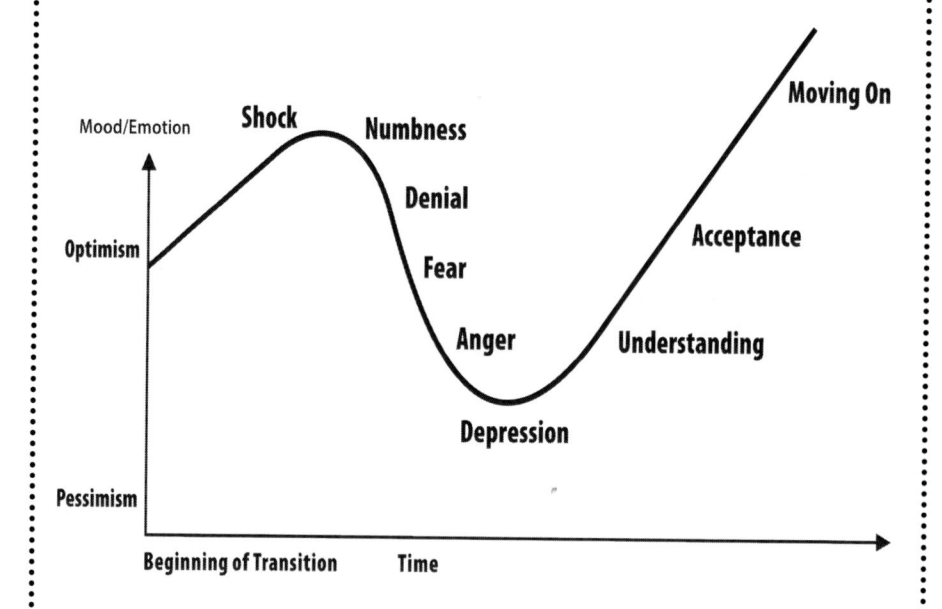

Mood/Emotion

Shock — Numbness — Denial — Fear — Anger — Depression — Understanding — Acceptance — Moving On

Optimism

Pessimism

Beginning of Transition — Time

WEEK 10

What positive things have you experienced in the last seven days?

- _____
- _____
- _____
- _____
- _____
- _____
- _____

How do you feel? Give yourself a score: **/10**

What is your goal for this week? Give a lot of details: what, where, when, what time, how, who with?

- _____
- _____
- _____
- _____
- _____
- _____
- _____

TECHNIQUES

What do the following techniques do?

- The "I Am Fantastic" Technique
- Depression Management Techniques
- The Calm Technique
- Anger Management Techniques
- The Swinnen Technique
- Sleeping Techniques
- Decision-Making Technique
- The ADKAR Technique

WEEK 11

What positive things have you experienced in the last seven days?

-
-
-
-
-
-
-

How do you feel? Give yourself a score: /10

What is your goal for this week? Give a lot of details: what, where, when, what time, how, who with?

-
-
-
-
-
-
-

Do more of what makes you Happy

WEEK 12

What positive things have you experienced in the last seven days?

- _____
- _____
- _____
- _____
- _____
- _____
- _____

How do you feel? Give yourself a score: **/10**

What is your goal for this week? Give a lot of details: what, where, when, what time, how, who with?

- _____
- _____
- _____
- _____
- _____
- _____
- _____

NOTES

ANSWERS

PUZZLE

1. Stress is not always bad.
2. The intellectual brain is positive.
3. The pre-frontal cortex is the boss.
4. The pre frontal cortex wants to achieve your goals.
5. Daydreaming is good for us.
6. The primitive brain is negative.
7. The primitive brain keeps us alive.
8. The amygdala is your bodyguard.
9. The hippocampus is your filing cabinet.
10. The hypothalamus is your chemist.

QUIZ 1

1. True	3. True	5. True	7. True	9. True
2. True	4. True	6. False	8. False	10. True

QUIZ 2

1. True	3. True	5. True	7. True	9. True
2. True	4. False	6. False	8. True	10. False

WHAT I GOT FROM THIS BOOK

Feelings	Knowledge

Ideas	Take Action

ACKNOWLEDGEMENTS

Mind for Better Health
Changing Minds Derbyshire
Mind Tools: Burnout Self-Test
Dr Barbara Oakley
Mayo Clinic
Robert Heller and Tim Hindle: Essential Manager's Manual
Vicky Hollett, Roger Carter, Liz Lyon, Emma Tanner: In At the Deep End
An Swinnen: The Business Survival Guide (because it's a jungle out there)
Unknown author at Penn State University: Time-Management-Central.net
Business Balls website
Elisabeth Kubler-Ross: Death and Dying
Jef Hiatt, Prosci: The ADKAR Model
Change Management Learning Centre
William Marston: DISC Personality Theory
PT Direct
National Health Service UK
CPHT Plymouth and Bristol
Donald Cadogan, Oak Tree Counceling
Wikipedia
123 Test
Cartoonstock.com
Nick Milton, Knoco Stories
University of Worcester
William Marston: The DISC Personalities
The Children's Trust, Brain Injury Hub
Tara Swart: The Unlimited Mind
Scott Jones: The brain Made Simple
Great Performers Academy
Helen Quach
Lauren Gelman, Reader's Digest
Florence Williams, National Geographic
Kerry-Anne Jennings, Health Line
Lisa Mosconi, The Alzheimer's Prevention Centre
Neuro Nation
Deborah Blum: Love at Goon Park
Harry Harlow: The Science of Affection.

S Cohen, D Janicki Deverts, R Turner: Does Hugging Provide Stress-Buffering Social Support?

L. C. Hawkley and J. T. Cacioppo: Loneliness Matters: A Theoretical and Empirical Review of Consequences and Mechanisms.

Deane Alban, Be Brain Fit

Florence Williams, Reader's Digest

Jason Murugesu, The New Statesman

Dr Phil Reed and Rhia Powell, Swansea University

Terry Martin and Sanja Jelic, Very Well Mind

Dr Richard D Hurt, Mayo Clinic Rochester

National Institute on Drug Abuse

Alice James and Louie Stowell: Looking After your Mental Health

Mark Aramli

Joe Griffin and Ivan Tyrell: Human Givens

Belle Beth Cooper, Buffer

Lawrence Robinson, Melinda Smith, M.A., and Jeanne Segal, Help Guide

Richard Bandler, Co-Founder of Neuro Linguistic Programming

Paul McKenna: Control Stress

Online College Organisation

Andy Workman: Cavemen and Polar Bears

Dr Barry J. Gibb: The Rough Guide to the Brain

Mark Connelly, Change Management Coach

iNews

The Atlantic

The Movie Database

Blissful Mind.com

Camille Newbold, Pinterest

Susan E. Hendrich

Ric LDP Artworks

To all neurologists, psychologists, psychiatrists, psychotherapists, doctors, scientists, researchers, authors, universities, hospitals, Ministries of Health and other organisations dedicated to understanding the brain and making us feel better. If you have been left out, it has not been done on purpose. I truly respect and acknowledge all of your work.

RELAXATION RECORDING

Surf to *www.becsltd.com* or *www.answinnen.com*
and go to the shop page.

Find the relaxation recording titled:

Brain Based Stress Management

Relaxation Recording

Type in the code which is:

TheSwinnenTechnique

Download the recording

Make sure you are somewhere safe and comfortable when you listen to the recording. Please do not drive or use tools or machinery while listening. Do not listen if you suffer from epilepsy. If in doubt, check with your doctor.

Listening to the recording several times a week will help you relax and sleep. Soon you will feel calmer, more positive and more self-confident.

ENJOY!!!

COMING SOON:

Brain Based Pain Management